S0-BAX-932

The Beginner's Bible Study Guide

The Complete Guide to Understanding the Old and New Testament

Learn the Fundamental Lessons of Jesus Christ

- SECOND EDITION -

By Dominique Atkinson

© **Copyright 2016**

All rights reserved. No part of this book may be reproduced or transmitted in any form or by any means, electronically or mechanically, including photocopy, recording, or by and information storage or retrieval system, without the written permission from the publisher, except in the case of brief quotations embodied in critical articles or reviews.

Trademarks are the property of their respective holders. When used, trademarks are for the benefit of the trademark owner only.

DISCLAIMER

The information provided herein is stated to be truthful and consistent, in that any liability, in terms of inattention or otherwise, by any usage or abusage of any policies, processes, or directions contained within is the solitary and utter responsibility of the recipient reader. Under no circumstances will any legal responsibility or blame be held against the publisher for any reparation, damages, or monetary loss due to the information herein, either directly or indirectly. Respective authors hold all rights not held by publisher.

Author's Note

In this book, we hope to help you connect with God on a more personal level by enhancing your knowledge of the Bible, Scriptures, Prayer, and Worship. We begin the book by reviewing a brief history of the origin and composition of the Bible, how the Bible was formed, and what the great influences of the times were that propagated change. We then offer an introduction to the Old and New Testament, including stories from Scripture that are part of the core of Christianity. We delineate specific theologies of God, Jesus, Jesus' saving work, prayer, forgiveness, and the Holy Spirit, perhaps the least understood part of the Trinity.

We have listed the chapters and books of the Bible chronologically, so that if someone wanted to study the Bible in order according to when it was lived, instead of when it has been listed in the Table of Contents of the Holy Bible, there is the opportunity to do so. Studying the Bible chronologically can help one make sense of the ever changing tableau when reading Kings and Chronicles. The Bible did not start out in written form; Judaism's roots come from a time when the oral tradition, rather than the written, was how a culture's memories were preserved. The New Testament had the advantage of being written before 150 AD, and by the middle of the third century, its 27 books were accepted as the foundation of the Christian experience.

We have suggested differing methods of Bible study, and proposed memorization of Scripture. We have recommended tried and true methods for Adult learning of Scriptures. We have a section on the importance of prayer and corporate worship. There are suggestions for a typical prayer and how to look for a home church or fellowship.

Finally, there is an index of helpful Scriptures to reference in times of personal trials and tribulations. Memorizing these Scriptures can offer a great comfort to one who is worried or at the end of their rope. Religious faith is based upon the knowledge that others have suffered as we suffered; have endured pain, loss, desperation and fear as we do, but throughout the human experience, God is with us.

We hope that you can utilize the material in the book to bring you to a closer relationship with God.

Dominique Atkinson

Table of Contents

Chapter 1: History of the Bible

The most common Bible used by Protestants within the United States is the 1626 edition of the King James Bible. This was not the first Bible to be published, and is not even the first edition of the King James Bible. This edition of the Bible was first commissioned in 1604, at the request of King James I, immediately after the death of Queen Elizabeth I. England had undergone a religious transformation which had altered the very fabric of the nation: in 1534, Henry VIII, miffed because the Pope had refused to grant him a divorce from Katherine of Aragon so that Henry could marry Anne Boleyn, declared himself the head of the Church of England. The subsequent years of Tudor rule were ones in which religion was a powerful and unruly undercurrent. The young King Edward VI was a staunch Protestant during whose brief reign the *Book of Common Prayer* became a cornerstone of the Reformation in England. When he died and his Catholic sister Mary I became queen, she restored England to the traditional faith and observed the primacy of the Pope. When Mary died, Protestant Elizabeth I was wary of religious extremism and sought, as much as she was able, to keep England free from the religious turmoil that could so easily turn into civil war.

When Elizabeth I died after a long and prosperous reign, the Tudor dynasty came to an end and the throne passed to their relatives, the Scottish Stuarts. England and Scotland were united and the Scottish James VI traveled south to become James I of Great Britain. Unlike his mother, Mary, Queen of Scots, who was Catholic, James had been brought up emphatically Protestant. But like Elizabeth, his predecessor, he was aware that whoever took the throne was beset by religious conflict. That conflict` also manifested itself in the versions of the Bibles which the English used. The Geneva Bible was based on the translation of William Tyndale, who was executed for heresy in 1536. However, Tyndale's Bible, a Puritan favorite, was not as popular with royalty because in the margin notes, Tyndale dared to express the opinions that kings were bound by rules. The Bishops' Bible, which had been translated in 1568, was produced because a Bible was needed, but it was a sloppy word done in haste and was not in common use.

King James wanted to appease the Protestants, the Pilgrims, and maintain separation from the Roman Catholics. King James was waylaid by a contingent of Puritans on his journey from Scotland to England to assume his new throne, who presented a petition for a proposed 1,000 changes to the Church of England. This petition was signed by more than 10% of the current clergy of England and Scotland, over 1,000 signatures, and so was named the Millenary Petition. Clearly, a country in need of a firm religious identity needed a Bible which was the irrefutable word of God.

This petition convinced King James to call the Hampton Court Conference of 1603. James assembled 54 biblical scholars who represented the existing range of theological beliefs from low-church Puritans up to those steeped in the elaborate ceremony of the Church of England. Divided into six groups, each was assigned to translate a section of the Bible. These theologians were by no means isolated ivory tower clerics unfamiliar with life. They were well traveled, they were scholarly and some were brilliant. But James' expectations were clear: the Bible was to be readily understood by the English. In the preface to the 1611 Bible, the translators wrote "We desire that the Scripture may speak like itself, that it may be understood even of the very vulgar."

The process was demanding. After the members of the individual groups finished translating their section of scripture, the group compared the versions against each other and decided on the one which best represented the Scriptural intent. A committee then listened to the selection as it was read aloud while they compared it to previous translations. The translations were discussed, and not only did the integrity of Scripture have to be maintained, but the literary quality had to measure up as well. When the final version was ready, it was reviewed by high ranking members of clergy, including the Archbishop of Canterbury and then to King James I. Dr. John Hall, a modern-day dean of Westminster, explains why the King James Bible is so powerful. "The language is full of mystery and grace, but it is also a version of loving authority, and that is the great message of this book."

In time, the King James Bible became the Holy Book which represented the English–speaking world's knowledge of their faith. It went to the New World with the Europeans who sought freedom in a land where there were no established traditions. American presidents have taken the oath of office by placing their hands upon the King James Bible. As it shaped religious identity, it shaped the English language.

This version was edited and revised several times until 1769. The 1769 Authorized Version is the King James Bible that is in use today. King James gave specific instructions to eliminate notes and passages he considered offensive, and to retain the hierarchy and patriarchy of the Church of England.

Before the King James Version, there was the Tyndale Bible and the Geneva Bible, among other popular versions. The Apocrypha was included in all of these editions until approximately 1769, at which time the publishers decided to remove this section to reduce printing costs and promote the sale of a cheaper product. Many current denominations still use the Apocrypha, including the United Methodists, the Episcopalians, the Presbyterians, the Roman Catholic Church, and the Orthodox churches.

The original compilation of the books of the Bible, called the canon, was decided by various persons throughout the first 500 years of church history. The Septuagint was a collection of Hebrew Scriptures made available in the 2nd Century. This was the original Bible for the Christian Church.

In the 4th century, at the Council of Laodicea, a simple canon was formed from the many copies of the Bible that were in circulation. Various books were discarded, including a third book of Corinthians, a continuation of Acts called the Acts of Paul and Thecla, and assorted books that portrayed women as disciples and leaders.

From this point, Jerome of the Roman Catholic Church was asked to translate the Bible into vernacular Latin, to make it more understandable for the clergy. The Latin vulgate of the Roman church became the Bible as it is understood today, mostly because no one else wanted to translate the Holy Scriptures. The Latin Vulgate was ratified and confirmed at the Council of Trent, in 1563. The Holy Bible was not divided into chapters or verses until the early 1600s, for the convenience of the printers.

There are various versions of the Bible still today. The Protestant

Church uses the King James version more than any other set of denominations, and only uses 66 books. The Jewish Bible is just 24 books and includes the Torah, the prophets, and the writings. The Ethiopian Orthodox Bible is the largest collection of Scriptures, with 81 books. The Bible is the bestselling book in the world; it's estimated that more than 3.9 billion copies have been sold. However this number fails to include the number of Bibles that have been given away. Although there is no way of being sure exactly how many Bibles are in existence, there is no doubt that this book is one of the most influential works of literature in human   civilization.

Chapter 2: The Old Testament

The Old Testament consists of 39 books for Protestants and 48 books for Catholics. The first five books of the Old Testament (called the Pentateuch) were written by four sources, although it was originally thought to be written by Moses. In the early 18th century this attribution became problematic when it was realized that in the book of Deuteronomy, Moses describes his own death. As this is particularly hard to do, theologians began to examine the texts and came to the agreement that there are four sources that wrote the Pentateuch, called the Documentary Hypothesis. This is the current understanding of the origination of the Pentateuch.

The Old Testament, or Hebrew Scriptures, is a continuous story of the creation of the world, and God's attempt to draw creation to God's self. The stories and interwoven tales of sin and redemption, man's condition of sinfulness, man's punishment by God, suffering and redemption, and God's grace and forgiveness all serve to demonstrate the mercy of God and God's desire to be in a relationship with humanity. The promise of a Messiah, or Savior, who will be sent by God to comfort his people has its roots in the Old Testament. For Christians, that promise is fulfilled when Jesus is born.

Even though the Old Testament had various authors and interpretations, there are recurring themes throughout the Hebrew Bible. All books are assumed to have been divinely inspired, written by God through the hands of men. The total meaning of the Bible is considered a mystery, to be pondered and studied to achieve relevance through the ages. All books of the Bible, including the Old Testament, show a just God, one of mercy and compassion. All of the books show that God is always ready for reconciliation with humankind, regardless of the acts of sin and depravity.

The Books of the Old Testament in Chronological Order

Genesis 1-10

Job 1-42

Genesis 11-50

Exodus 1-40

Leviticus 1-23

Numbers 1-36

Psalm 90

Joshua 1-24

Judges 17-21

Judges 1-8

Ruth 1-4

Judges 9-10

1 Samuel 1-2

Judges 11-16

1 Samuel 3-20

Psalm 59

1 Samuel 21

Psalm 52

Psalm 34

Psalm 56

1 Samuel 22

Psalm 57, 142

1 Samuel 23-2 Samuel 4

1 Chronicles 1-10

2 Samuel 5

1 Chronicles 11-14

2 Samuel 6

1 Chronicles 15

2 Samuel 7-8

Psalm 60, 15, 24

1 Chronicles 16

Psalm 96, 105, 106

1 Chronicles 17-18

2 Samuel 9-10

1 Chronicles 19-20

2 Samuel 11-12

Psalm 51

2 Samuel 12-14

Psalm 2-145, assorted

1 Chronicles 21-27

2 Samuel 15-16

Psalm 63

2 Samuel 17

Psalm 41, 55

2 Samuel 18-23

Psalm 108

2 Samuel 24

1 Chronicles 28-29

1 Kings 1-2

Psalm 37, 72

2 Chronicles 1

1 Kings 3

Psalm 45

1 Kings 4-9

2 Chronicles 2-7

Psalm 135, 136

2 Chronicles 8

Psalm 127

Proverbs 1-31

Songs 1-8

1 Kings 9-10

2 Chronicles 9

1 Kings 11

Ecclesiastes 1-12

1 Kings 11:40-13

2 Chronicles 10-12

1 Kings 14-15

2 Chronicles 13-14

1 Kings 16

2 Chronicles 15-16

1 Kings 16

2 Chronicles 17

1 Kings 17-22

Obadiah 1

2 Chronicles 18-21

2 Kings 1-11

2 Chronicles 22-24

2 Kings 12

Joel 1-3

2 Kings 12:6-14

2 Chronicles 25

2 Kings 15

2 Chronicles 26

Amos 1-9

Jonah 1-4

Hosea 1-14

2 Chronicles 27-28

Isaiah 1-7

Micah 1-7

Isaiah 8-35

2 Kings 17

2 Chronicles 29-31

2 Kings 20

Isaiah 38-66

2 Kings 18

2 Chronicles 32

Psalms 46-48

2 Kings 19

Isaiah 37

Nahum 1-3

2 Kings 21

2 Chronicles 33

2 Kings 22

2 Chronicles 34

Zephaniah 1-3

Jeremiah 1-10

Habakkuk 1-3

Jeremiah 11-12

2 Kings 22-23

2 Chronicles 35-36

Jeremiah 13-20, 46-47

Daniel 1-2

2 Kings 24

Jeremiah 48-49

Ezekiel 1-23

2 Kings 25

Jeremiah 21-45

Ezekiel 24-25

Jeremiah 52

Psalms 74, 79

Jeremiah 50-51

Lamentations 1-5

Ezekiel 26-39

Daniel 3-4

Ezekiel 40-48

Daniel 5-12

Ezra 1-5

Haggai 1,2

Zechariah 1-14

Ezra 6

Esther 1-10

Ezra 7-10

Nehemiah 1-13

Malachi 1-4

The Most Important Stories of the Old Testament

The Creation Story

This is the story of the creation of the world by God. In this story, God creates the universe, and all that is within it out of nothingness. In the beginning God. That's how the first book of the Bible, Genesis, begins, with an explanation of the Creation. God moves upon the void and separates light and darkness, he forms the oceans and the land mass; creates the sun and the moon and the stars; the creatures of the water and air and land. On the sixth day, God created humanity. After the first six days, God rests, and instructs humankind in Exodus to also rest on the seventh day. This is the foundational Bible story because it demonstrates that God is primary and the source of all creation. God who is without beginning or end, created our world and humanity.

The Story of the Fall of Mankind

God and mankind dwelled in the Garden of Eden in loving harmony until the influence of sin was introduced by the serpent. They are provided a paradise in which to live, the Garden of Eden. The only rule that God requires is that they abstain from eating from the Tree of the Knowledge of Good and Evil. But when the serpent enters Eden, he has no trouble convincing the woman that eating the forbidden fruit will bring her wisdom, not punishment. She shares the fruit with her husband. The couple realizes that they are naked, and they try to hide from God. Adam and Eve are banished for their disobedience: the man is condemned to earning his living from the land, which will resist his efforts to tame it. The woman will give birth in pain. From their act of disobedience, the inclination to sin becomes part of the human character.

Once sin is introduced, humanity is flawed through the disobedience of Adam and Eve (known as original sin). The concept of original sin is the doctrine that humanity is corrupted through the original sin of Adam and Eve, "**12** Wherefore, as by one man sin entered into the world, and death by sin; and so death passed upon all men, for that all have sinned:" Romans 5:12. After disobeying God, Adam and Eve were banished from the Garden of Eden and forced to work and travail all of their lives.

The Story of Cain and Abel

The Book of Genesis takes place during a time when the roadmap for wrongdoing is still being written. The first murder takes place as a jealous Cain kills his brother Abel, whose sacrifice to God is more pleasing. Cain faces banishment for his sin; though the Ten Commandments had not yet been delivered to Moses, the

23

assumption in the early books is that humans knew right from wrong, and murder numbered among the sins to be punished.

But even in his punishment, when he is banished east of Eden, Cain calls on God to rescue him, fearing that the populations of other communities (whose origins are not explained) will kill him. God marks him to save him, showing the divine clemency which throughout the Bible is God's trademark: his people fall short of his will and sin against him, and despite his anger, his love for them surmounts his disappointment.

The Story of the Rainbow

The early world of the Bible is a rough, raw place. From their nearness to God, the ancient Israelites eventually become so infested with sin that God must destroy his creation. Only Noah is deemed worthy of salvation and he is instructed to build an ark. While his neighbors mock him for his presumed folly, Noah goes on building. The ark is populated with his wife, his sons and their wives, and multiples of God's animals so that when the world is restored to wholeness, the nucleus of the original creation will be present. Noah obeys God's command and as the waters flood the entire earth and drown all its inhabitants, those inside the ark are safe. After 40 days and nights of sailing upon the surging waters of the sodden world, the ark arrives on dry land. God promises that never again will he destroy the world with water; his promise is marked by the rainbow.

The Tower of Babel

Despite getting a second chance after the Great Flood that destroyed the original creation, the human race failed to learn its lesson. At this time, Genesis explains, the entire world spoke one language. The people decided to build a tower that reached to the heavens. But God was not pleased by this ambition. Instead of one language, there were suddenly many, an interesting reversal of what would happen at Pentecost in the New Testament. The people were scattered all over the earth and the heavens were secure.

The Covenant with Abraham

The rainbow is the mark of a covenant between God and his people. The covenant is further defined generations later when God calls Abraham out of the land of Ur. God will make of Abraham and his descendants a mighty nation, so numerous that they cannot be counted. Abraham, mindful of his childless state, his advanced age and his elderly wife, is dubious, but devout. He follows God's lead and travels from his home to the land of Canaan, which will become the Promised Land. Abraham prospers, but remains childless. God's promise of an heir seems distant. Abraham finally fathers a son, but with his wife's handmaiden, Hagar. Sarah is jealous and orders the woman and her son, the reminder of Sarah's infertility, to be banished. Abraham does as she orders (for all that it is a patriarchal society, there are significant instances where the men of the ruling tents bend to the will of the women in their lives). But God takes pity on Hagar and Ishmael, and does not let them die; Ishmael, he vows, will become a nation. Muslims believe that the Prophet Mohammed is descended from the line of Ishmael.

Jacob the Trickster

Sarah does produce a son, Isaac, who marries Rebecca, and they become the parents of the battling twins, Esau the elder, and

Jacob, Rebecca's favorite, who cheats Esau out of his birthright as the eldest and is forced to flee for his life. He escapes to his uncle Laban's lands, where he falls in love with Laban's daughter Rachel. He first marries, through Laban's trickery (deceit was a family trait), the elder daughter Leah, then works another seven years so that he can claim Rachel as his wife. He also takes, as concubines, the maids of his wives. From his wives and concubines, Jacob fathers 12 sons who become the 12 tribes of Israel.

Joseph

Jacob prefers Joseph, his first son with his beloved Rachel, over all his other sons, and the 11 brother's tire of Joseph's favored son status, especially when their father gifts Joseph with a coat of many colors. They sell him into slavery and tell Jacob that he's dead. Joseph eventually becomes the right-hand man of the Egyptian pharaoh, and the steward of the vast agricultural wealth of the kingdom. When famine hits the region, the sons of Jacob go to Egypt to seek food, not knowing that the brother they sold into slavery is now a favorite once again, this time to the pharaoh, and a man of great power.. The family reconciles and all move to Egypt to share in the restored son's prosperity, including Jacob, who rejoices that the son he thought was dead is alive.

The Israelites in Egypt

But then there arose a pharaoh "who knew not Joseph." The Israelites are made slaves, forced to labor in building the Egyptian monarchy's architectural wonders. From the Hebrew people arises a rescuer named Moses who is raised in Pharaoh's court. But when Moses commits murder and must escape, he leaves Egypt. He becomes a shepherd, marries, and seems to have forgotten his royal past. Until one day, when he detects a bush that, although afire, doesn't burn. Curious, Moses creeps closer and is introduced to God.

Moses

God has a mission for Moses: Tell Pharaoh to let my people go. Moses is reluctant; he's slow of speech, disinclined to return to the land he left under a cloud, and not at all sure that the Israelites will have a clue what he's talking about. After all, who is God? God says, "Tell them, I Am." and with those cryptic instructions and God's permission to take his smooth-talking brother Aaron with him, Moses returns to Egypt. It takes a plethora of bloody rivers, frogs, lice, flies, pestilence, boils, hail, darkness, locusts, and finally, the death of all the firstborn of Egypt, but Pharaoh capitulates: the Israelites may go.

The First Passover

The first Passover is the story of the deliverance of the Israelites from the hand of Pharaoh in Egypt. Pharaoh continued to hold the Jewish people in captivity despite the plagues that had been visited upon the Egyptians at the hands of the Hebrew God. God told the people to mark their doorposts with the blood of the lamb, and He would send the Angel of Death to take the life of every firstborn son, include the son of Pharaoh. The Angel of Death struck at the households of the Egyptians, where the firstborn of the land, from sons to livestock, were found dead. This was the last of the ten plagues necessary to soften the heart of Pharaoh, and let God's people go.

But then Pharaoh changes his mind, as he was prone to do. When he, his soldiers and chariots are drawing near to the Israelites who are at the shore of the Red Sea, Moses raises his staff; the waters part and the Israelites cross to dry land. But as the Egyptians prepare to cross, the wall of water engulfs them and they drown. God's mission to save his people has been accomplished.

The re-enactment of the Passover is celebrated every year by Jews worldwide in a special meal, called Seder. In addition, this Scripture passage is a precursor to the necessity of purification by the blood of a lamb, which for Christians, is represented through Jesus Christ. Jesus Christ, while entering into Jerusalem, celebrated the Passover at the Last Supper and reminded his disciples that his body and blood were being sacrificed for them. Jesus was born a Jew and died a Jew. After the establishment of the Christian religion, the Passover became the Eucharist, celebrated in remembrance of the Last Supper that Jesus shared with his disciples before his arrest, crucifixion, and death.

The Ten Commandments

For 40 years, the quarreling, complaining people of God wander in the wilderness, lamenting the loss of their home, forgetting that they were slaves and are now free. Freedom seems less important than their memories of the food they left behind in Egypt and their regrets at leaving seem to be endless. Moses seeks to construct a nation from these former slaves. He meets with God on Mt. Sinai and comes down the mountain with stone tablets upon which are inscribed the Ten Commandments, the basis for what will become the Jewish code of law. There's a bit of unpleasantness over a golden calf; frightened by Moses' absence, the Israelites decide that melting down their gold and creating a substitute god will comfort them. Moses doesn't handle this well, breaks the stone tablets and has to return to Sinai to get a replacement set.

With order restored, the Ten Commandments are delivered. The remaining three books of the law in the Torah are an exhaustive catalogue of the laws, rules, codified statutes, governing principles and sacred practices of what will transform the wandering-in-the-wilderness people of Israel into a consolidated nation whose history will eventually take them to the heights of power and the depths of subjugation, but will nonetheless maintain their identity as the chosen people of God.

Delivered from slavery in Egypt and provided with a code of law to live by, the nation of Israel looked to new leaders to replace Moses, who died without entering Canaan. The torch is first passed to Joshua, who knew Egyptian enslavement, the wandering for 40 years, and the arrival to the land of milk and honey, the Promised Land. Israel goes through a cycle of leaders, beginning with the heroic Joshua, then to the various judges who rule in a semi-prophetic, semi-judicial manner, until the nation looks to kings to lead them.

The Next Generation of Leaders

The Books of History are an account of the leaders of Israel, the battle commanders, judges, prophets, and kings who are prominent in the growing years of nationhood. But the books also include the only two books in the Bible named for women: Ruth, who was not an Israelite, and Esther, the story of a Jewish girl who saved her people. The books of history begin with Joshua's assumption of the mantle of leadership and his success as a military commander, bringing Israel to triumph over her enemies, delivering the Promised Land of Canaan to the Israelites, and destroying Jericho with his marching and trumpet playing until the walls fell.

Joshua believed that the Israelites could overcome all their enemies and claim the kingdom that God had promised them. Under his leadership, they were cohesive, but after his death, the absence of a strong leader for a people who had relied on men with close ties to God, and the lack of a defined governing structure, weaken the nation. The 12 tribes are not united. Beyond Israel's borders are ancient enemies whose religious practices are at odds with the monotheistic tenets of Judaism. God is furious with his people's failure to obey, and moved to pity when they are overwhelmed by the consequences of their acts. The scripture verse from Judges 21:25: "In these days there was no king in Israel. Everyone did what was right in his own eyes" was an indictment of the people's tendency to sin and the failure of the religious leaders to hold them in check.

Joshua believed that the Israelites could overcome all their enemies and claim the kingdom that God had promised them. Under his leadership, they were cohesive, but after his death, the absence of a strong leader for a people who had relied on men with close ties to God, and the lack of a defined governing structure, weaken the nation. The 12 tribes are not united. Beyond Israel's borders are ancient enemies whose religious practices are at odds with the monotheistic tenets of Judaism. God is furious with his people's failure to obey, and moved to pity when they are overwhelmed by the consequences of their acts. The scripture verse from Judges 21:25: "In these days there was no king in Israel. Everyone did what was right in his own eyes" was an indictment of the people's tendency to sin and the failure of the religious leaders to hold them in check.

Despite the title of the book, the judges who ruled Israel during this period of time demonstrated relatively few judicial qualities.

Samson, he of the "brawn and no brains" style of leadership, was an easy mark for a calculating woman like Delilah, who learned the secret of his strength (his might came from the fact that his hair had never been cut) after multiple failed attempts to tease and coax the answer from him. Upon learning it, she took scissors to his locks, and allowed the Philistines to capture him and blind him. In one last act of strength, as his hair begins to grow back, Samson pulls down the columns of the Philistine temple, killing many of his nation's foes.

In an interesting twist for a patriarchal nation, one of the most reputable judges was a woman. Deborah dispensed justice and wisdom and, when the Hebrew people head to war, the commander Barak refuses to go into battle until the prophetess goes with him. Deborah warns him that for his doubts, the credit for the victory in battle would not be his, but would belong to a woman. The Israelites win and enjoy peace for 40 years. Some of their judges display wisdom and rule according to God, others prove to be less than stellar.

Israel Wants a King

Eventually, however, Israel wanted what the other nations had: a king. Their first king, Saul, is chosen because he was taller than most men (proving that people throughout history have had shallow reasons for their political loyalty), but Saul turns out to be flawed. His path and that of a young shepherd named David cross when the Philistine warrior Goliath challenges the Israelite troops to meet him in man-to-man combat. None of the Israelites wants to face the giant.

The Story of David and Goliath

The story of David defeating the giant Goliath is not just the story of a boy becoming a hero for the Israelites, it is also more importantly the story of mankind relying on God to solve problems that seem insurmountable in the eyes of the world. Even though David did defeat the best warrior, Goliath, with a humble slingshot, the primary focus of this story should be that God takes the willing heart rather than the obviously powerful as his instruments to use in the Kingdom of God.

For Christians, this is the story of faith in God to remind us to utilize our meager resources and our mustard seed of faith to destroy the evil in our world.

David was a gifted man, a powerful leader, a talented musician. He also had an eye for the ladies. One in particular, Bathsheba, was the wife of another man, but that was not an obstacle for a king. David summons her to his chambers, and orders her husband sent to the front of the battle. Death for Uriah in the most intense part of the battle soon follows, allowing David to claim Bathsheba as his wife, or rather one of them, monogamy not being a notable characteristic of monarchs at this period of time.

The prophet Nathan warns David that God is not pleased with what he did to obtain Bathsheba and that, because of it, his household will be one of strife. David's domestic life is filled with discord; David's eldest son Amnon rapes David's daughter Tamar and goes unpunished. Tamar's brother Absalom has his half-brother killed for revenge. Absalom was a favorite of David and of the people, but the damage is done. Absalom revolts against David and, fleeing from battle, Absalom's splendid head of hair turns into his downfall: his locks become entangled in the branches of a tree and David's commander Joab kills him, opting for civil order rather than the forgiving love of an unwise parent.

David's Heirs

By birth, the next king should have been Adonijah, the next in line, but when David becomes old and infirm, Bathsheba goes to the king to ensure that her son Solomon will be named king. She has the support of the prophet Nathan, and Solomon is immediately proclaimed king while his father is alive. Solomon's reign begins well. He asks God for wisdom in his rule rather than riches or long life. Solomon's reputation for wisdom is so renowned that the Queen of Sheba comes to visit him, bringing with her gold, spices, and jewels.

To Solomon, God gives permission to build the temple at Jerusalem, which would become a symbol of the nation of Israel's faith and power. Solomon, like his father, enjoyed the company of the fair sex, so much so that he marries 700 of them and has, in addition, 300 concubines. Many of his wives were foreign princesses who worshipped other gods. In time, their beliefs infiltrate his own and he builds temples for their gods. God's punishment for this violation will split the kingdom apart during the reign of Solomon's son Rehoboam. The ten tribes of Israel in the north reject Rehoboam as king and become the kingdom of Israel. Rehoboam ruled as king of Judah, in the south. Only three kings—Saul, David, and Solomon—reigned over a united Israel. For the next two centuries, the northern and southern kingdoms have separate kings. The history of the Israelite monarchy is not one of wise and judicious governance. The verse "He did evil in the eyes of the Lord, just as his predecessors had done" becomes the litany of the royal line.

In 722 BCE, the Assyrians, led by King Sennacherib, conquer Israel, taking its citizens into captivity. Although he brings his forces against Judah and besieges its capital, Jerusalem, he does not capture the city. Judah's King Hezekiah calls on the protection of God; the prophet Isaiah, one of the major prophets of the Old Testament, is a vital force in the life of the kingdom.

Widely regarded as the most evil of all the queens who married into the Israelite royal family, Jezebel, wife of King Ahab, came to a particularly gruesome fate for her sins. She was thrown from a window; when the king who ordered her death sent his servants to bury her, all that was left was her skull, feet, the palms of her hands, and her blood. The dogs, as predicted by the prophet Elijah, had devoured her.

The Exile

But the times were out of joint for the Israelite people. Nebuchadnezzar of Babylon conquers Judah in 597 BCE, taking many of the Israelites into captivity. Political jockeying was a way of life for kings and their advisors; King Zedekiah, ignoring the advice of the prophet Jeremiah, sides with Egypt and revolts against the Babylonians. Nebuchadnezzar's retaliation is swift and bloody; he destroys Jerusalem and its temple, blinds the king and murders his sons, and takes many of the country's citizens back with him to Babylon, including the prophet Ezekiel. The prophet Daniel is also taken to Babylon where he becomes a royal favorite. But the independent kingdom of Judah was no more.

The time of exile, while a tragedy for the nation, is nonetheless a time of transformational development in the life of Judaism. The Torah, the five books of the law, became the authoritative text for the Jewish faith. The exile meant the end of the tribes as a means of identifying the Israelites, except for the tribe of Levi, the priests, which continued to represent the priestly role in the nation and care for the temple. The phrase Diaspora, referring to the Jews who did not live in the land of Israel or Judah, becomes a point of reference for the population.

When the Persian King Cyrus conquers Babylon in 539 BCE, the exile to Babylon ends. Cyrus allows the Jews to return home, and encourages the rebuilding of the temple. Under the direction of Nehemiah, the prophet, the temple rebuilding began.

The Psalms

Known as the Books of Wisdom, the five books which follow the books of history are remarkable for their eloquence. And, perhaps, for their respite; it's as if, after the bloody tragedies and violence of the nation's history, the Bible needs time to rest. The Psalms praise God, berate God, question God, and submit to God. They are remarkable for their candor. They are said to have been written by King David, who, when he wasn't tending sheep, cold-cocking giants, and marrying attractive and fertile women, played a mean harp. David's psalms convey the gamut of human responses to God, and at no point is there any indication that one needs to hold back. What one feels in faith, one can express. God's love is infinite.

Job

The Book of Job, in which God and Satan place a bet on whether God's faithful servant will continue to worship God despite trials and tribulations, tells the saga of a good man who is beset by troubles through no fault of his own. The book, which if it were to be written today would be subtitled *Why do Really Bad Things Happen to a Really Good Person?* concludes with a stirring defense by God of his own actions, and his unfathomability, as well as a defense of Job.

Of all the Books of Wisdom, readers and believers struggle the most with the character of Job, a good, godly man whose punishment and loss seems to be inflicted upon him by a divine whim. God affirms that Job is a good man who has done no wrong and yet is punished miserably. God responds to Job, but does not offer a reason for Job's suffering. Regarded as an allegory, the Book of Job nonetheless offers a bitter comfort for believers who feel that their suffering is undeserved, but know that God has not forgotten them.

Proverbs to Live By

The Book of Proverbs is a lesson in life, imparted by an older, wiser, and somewhat stuffier man to a young one. In many ways it reminds the reader of Polonius, who delivers his counsel to his son Laertes in Shakespeare's *Hamlet*. But the book encourages the young man to follow God, to seek wisdom, and in so doing, to strive to live a moral life in keeping with God's teachings. Had the writer lived in modern times, the book would have been a merchandising gold mine, with calendars, tee-shirts and coasters supplementing the verses. In its original version, it seeks to keep young people on the path of virtue by warning them of what awaits if they stray from God.

The Song of Solomon

The presence of the Song of Solomon in the Bible at all is somewhat of an eye-opener. There are those scholars who affirm that it's an allegorical account of the bonds between God and Israel. Likewise, some Christian thought holds that the book, also known as the Song of Songs, relates the nature of the love between Jesus, who in the New Testament is portrayed as the bridegroom, and his bride, the Church. The passages don't refer to God or to matters of faith. Instead, the book is a passionate affirmation of the beauty of sexual love. The lovers praise each other with ardent compliments and affirmations of their intense affection. Although Solomon is credited with its authorship, linguistic evidence indicates that it was likely written long after Solomon's reign.

Ecclesiastes

The Book of Ecclesiastes, is credited to Solomon, but like Proverbs and the Song of Solomon, was also likely written long after David's son ruled as king. The book presents an almost ironic counterpoint to Proverbs, which lists a series of rules by which men and women should live. In Ecclesiastes, life is meaningless. Its purpose is not one of religious instruction, although it does begin with advice to keep the commandments of God. The author is addressing the frustration of life, which inescapably ends in death, and is marked throughout by loss and suffering. Despite its melancholy theme, the writing is evocative and eloquent.

In the ancient world, particularly the Near East, the tradition of wisdom literature was a literary way to impart moral teachings. In the Bible's Books of Wisdom, it's not events that are recounted. Rather, it's the thoughts and feelings of the people. In the Books of Wisdom, Wisdom is personified as female, God's companion, present at the time of the Creation.

The Prophets

The prophets of Israel and Judah had a thankless job. They were called by God to accuse the Israelites of their wrongdoing. Calling a nation to account for the sins it has committed, and doing so as the mouthpiece of God, is a surefire way to lose friends. The prophets took their work very seriously; they were the spiritual litmus test by which subsequent generations judged the willingness of their ancestors to heed the warnings which the prophets issued. Israel had had prophets since its early days; Moses is regarded as a prophet unlike any other; the Bible even says that no other prophet was like him, because God knew Moses face to face. A prophet was charged with warning the people that their sins had consequences. Prophets challenged the might of kings and faced the hostility of the people for their blunt speech. But, even more than its kings or its heroes, the prophets of Israel defined the nation.

Prophets were an integral part of the Israelite nation's history from its formation after enslavement thorough the time of Malachi in 420 BCE. However, the major and minor prophets whose works are included in the Old Testament spanned the years from approximately 800 to 400 BCE. Two of the prophets, Obadiah and Joel, fail to provide evidence for their period of prophecy and their time cannot be pinpointed. Some of the others, because their prophetic period was intermingled with times of great political activity, are easy to place in a chronology.

The four major prophets earned their adjective because of the volume of their writings: the works of Isaiah, Jeremiah, Ezekiel and Daniel comprise 183 chapters. We tend to think of these four major prophets as occupying a symbolic Mount Rushmore of prophecy. The writings of the 12 minor prophets total 67 chapters. The Old Testament books of the prophets also foretold events in the New Testament: Isaiah predicted the arrival of Jesus Christ; Ezekiel, Daniel and Zechariah predict Christ's return. Each prophet had a unique role to play in the history of the Jewish people. Isaiah is the longest of the books written by the major prophets, with 66 chapters, while the shortest book by minor prophet Obadiah consists of a single chapter.

Isaiah by anyone's standards is a legend in prophecy. He prophesied during the reign of Kings Jotham, Ahaz, and Hezekiah, and provided advice for Hezekiah that helped to save Jerusalem when Assyria's King Sennacherib besieged the city. However, when Hezekiah's heir came to the throne in 686 BCE, Jewish tradition says that the prophet was killed.

Jeremiah, author of the Books of Jeremiah and Lamentations, rose to answer God's call at a young age, possibly when he was less than 20 years old. At times he is forced to go into hiding and at one point, he was imprisoned by King Zedekiah as a traitor for recommending that the king surrender to the Babylonians. Jeremiah ends up in Egypt and probably died there, possibly stoned by his own people.

Ezekiel, the scion of a priestly family from Jerusalem, is taken into exile when Nebuchadnezzar conquered Judah in 597 BCE. He's famous for his seven visions; one of the most famous is his vision of the valley of the dry bones which heralds the restoration of Israel.

Daniel gained the attention of King Nebuchadnezzar in 603 BCE and became a trusted counselor. He incurs the jealousy of the other Babylonian counselors, but is saved by God's intervention from the fiery furnace into which he and his three friends are placed as a result of the machinations of the king's advisors. In this story, Meshach, Shadrach and Abednego are thrust into the fiery furnace for disobeying King Nebuchadnezzar's orders to bow down and worship the king's appointed idol at the sound of the trumpets and coronets. Meshach, Shadrach and Abednego were accused of not worshiping the king's idol. The king ordered the men to be thrown into a furnace 10 times the normal temperature of the fire. When the king looked into the furnace he saw four men, including the image of the Son of God. The three faithful Jewish young men were spared and Christians were given a glimpse of the pre-incarnate Jesus.

Daniel would again be saved, this time under the reign of the Persian King Cyrus, from the lion's den. The story of his faith during the Exile is a portent of what will happen to the Jews during the Diaspora, when they remain steadfast to their beliefs despite separation from their country and the oppression that they must endure.

The Book of Daniel contains several phrases which continue to have meaning in modern times. The "handwriting on the wall" refers to Chapter 5's words written by a disembodied hand upon the walls of the Babylonian king's palace. Daniel is called to interpret the writing; he explains that the words mean that the Babylonian kingdom will come to an end at the conquering hands of the Persians.

Daniel also interprets another biblical phrase "You have been weighed in the balance and found wanting." It's an indictment of Belshazzar, the grandson of Nebuchadnezzar, who allowed his dinner guests to drink from cups taken from the Jewish temple.

Minor prophets Hosea and Amos were contemporaries of one another. Hosea's preaching and his personal life are intertwined as his marriage to the prostitute Gomer reflects the nation's infidelity to God. Amos, a herdsman and not a priest, uses everyday terms to deliver God's message. He preaches that God plans to judge Israel by a plumb line to determine whether the nation is upright. God's patience has come to an end.

Joel's prophecy is undated but his prediction that although the land has suffered devastation by locust swarms (either actual or apocalyptic) and drought, repentance will restore God's blessing. God promises that, in the last days, his spirit will be poured out upon the people; the sons and daughters will prophecy, the old men will dream dreams, the young men will see visions.

Also undated, Obadiah's brief message of 21 verses preaches against the arrogance of the Edomites, descendants of Esau, the son of Isaac. The Edomites had helped Babylon loot the city of Jerusalem and Obadiah warns that God will rescue the Israelites but will destroy the house of Esau.

Jonah may be one of the most famous of all the prophets, thanks to the time he spent in the belly of a whale. His time of prophecy is estimated to be earlier, around 790 BCE. Jonah is sent to tell the city of Nineveh to repent. His reluctance to do so is what lands him inside the whale. Ultimately he does deliver God's message and the city is saved because its people repent of their sins.

Micah, whose time of prophecy began around 740 BCE, makes reference to images beloved of peacemakers everywhere when he says that God will settle the nations' disputes, and people will beat their swords into plowshares and their spears into pruning hooks.

Nahum preached early in the 600s BCE. Once again Nineveh is in the spotlight, but this time the outcome is not so promising.

Nineveh was the capital of the Assyrians, who had conquered Israel in 722 BCE. Nahum's prophecy warns them that what goes around, come around: their cruelty and idolatry will lead to their destruction at the hands of Babylon.

Habakkuk preached before the Babylonians destroyed Jerusalem in 586 BCE but his prophecies warn that they will be a rising power in the region.

Zephaniah, a possible contemporary of Habakkuk who may have had connections to the royal line of Hezekiah, preaches about the sin and idolatry of Judah at a time before King Josiah had begun his religious reforms.

Haggai's time of prophecy takes place in 520 BCE, during the rebuilding of the temple in Jerusalem, which was supported by the Persian King Darius the Great. The rebuilding of the temple began when the Jews were allowed to return to Judah, but the work was halted for a number of years because of hostile activity from the Samaritans, who had lived in the area before the exiled Jews returned.

Zechariah begins to prophecy in 520 BCE. Like Haggai, he encouraged the rebuilding of the temple. His prophecies also refer to the future of Jerusalem.

Malachi is preaching around 425 BCE, a time when the temple has already been rebuilt and religious rituals are once again taking place. Judah is ruled by a governor who answers to the Persian king. Malachi is warning the people that they are failing to observe the proper religious practices and are not faithful to God.

Chapter 3: The New Testament

The New Testament is a compilation of the stories of the life and significance of Jesus Christ, as told by first and second hand observers and followers. Jesus himself did not write any books of the Bible. Most of the writings of the New Testament were written by the Apostle Paul, although he never personally met Jesus face to face. (Paul was a converted Jew who persecuted Christians until God persuaded him to follow the teachings of Jesus Christ.) Early Christians wrote of the teachings of Christ but Paul wrote his interpretations of the life, death, and resurrection of Jesus Christ and its purpose for humanity.

The Books of the New Testament in Chronological Order

Luke 1

John 1

Luke 2

Matthew 1

Mark 1

Luke 2:6

John 1:14

Matthew 2

Matthew 2:13

Matthew 2:16

Matthew 2:23

Matthew 3

Luke 2:41

Mark 1:4

Luke 3

John 1:15

Matthew 3:13

Mark 1:9

Luke 3:21

Matthew 4

Mark 1:12

Luke 4

Matthew 4:18

Mark 1:16

Luke 5

John 2

John 3

John 4

Matthew 5-7

Luke 11

Matthew 8

Mark 2

Luke 4:14

John 5

Matthew 12

Mark 3

Luke 6

Matthew 11

Luke 7

Matthew 13

Mark 4

Luke 8

Matthew 8:28

Mark 5

Luke 8:26

Matthew 9

Matthew 10

Mark 6

Matthew 14

Mark 6:14

Matthew 14:15

Mark 6:30

Luke 9

John 6

Matthew 15

Mark 7

Matthew 16

Mark 8

Luke 9:18

Matthew 17

Mark 9

Luke 9:28

Matthew 18

Luke 10

John 7

John 8

John 9

John 10

Luke 12-16

Luke 17

John 11

Matthew 19, 20

Mark 10

Luke 18

Matthew 21

Mark 11

Luke 19

John 12

Matthew 22-25

Mark 12-13

Luke 20-21

Matthew 26

Mark 14

Luke 22

John 13

John 14

John 15

John 16

John 17

Matthew 27

Mark 15

Luke 23

John 18-19

Matthew 28

Mark 16

Luke 24

John 20-21

Acts 1-12

James 1-5

Acts 13-18

1 Thess. 1-5

2 Thess. 1-3

Acts 19

1 Cor. 1-16

Gal. 1-6

Acts 20

Romans 1-16

2 Cor. 1-13

Acts 21-28

Ephesians 1-6

Philippians 1-4

Colossians 1-4

Philemon 1

1 Timothy 1-6

1 Peter 1-5

Titus 1-3

2 Timothy 1-4

2 Peter 1-3

Hebrews 1-13

Jude 1

1 John 1-5

2 John 1

3 John 1

Revelation 1-22

The Most Important Stories of the New Testament

The gospels of Matthew, Mark, Luke, and John tell the story of the birth, life, death, and resurrection of Jesus of Nazareth. Gospel means "good news" and for the followers of the obscure Galilean named Jesus whose earthly life came to so violent and untimely end, the story of his resurrection was good news indeed. Each gospel has a different emphasis which, collectively, give us an account of the 33 years that Jesus, born in Bethlehem to Mary and her husband Joseph, spent in life and ministry before he was arrested, crucified, and placed in a tomb. Had the story ended there, it would have been worthy but not remarkable. Nor would it have fulfilled the Old Testament prophecies which predicted the birth of a king, a Messiah, who would deliver his people. For the long-suffering Jews who were living under the occupation of the Roman Empire, deliverance was assumed to be a military one. But followers of the Christ had to come to terms with the fact that the Messiah had come in peace to a world gripped by war. He was a victim of its violence, but he also transcended it. For many Jews, this was not the Messiah they had long awaited. For others, Jesus was the Son of God.

The Birth of the Messiah

The gospel of Matthew, written approximately a decade after the gospel of Mark, begins not in the immediate present like Mark does but in the far past, all the way back to Adam. Matthew is establishing the genealogy of Jesus, and to do that, he traces

Jesus' ancestry all the way back to creation. What's interesting in his tracking, in addition to the fact that Jesus' birth line includes the prostitute Rahab, is that he traces the line of Jesus not through his mother Mary, the virgin, but through her husband, Joseph. Jesus comes from the line of David, the warrior king and his genealogy includes, in addition to Rahab, Tamar, Ruth, and Bathsheba, noteworthy because these women achieved names in the Old Testament, which was not always the case, and also because of the inclusiveness which Jesus showed to women who participated in his ministry.

The story of the birth of Jesus Christ, the Messiah, is the foundational starting point for Christians. Without Christ, there is no reconciliation to God through forgiveness. Without the fully human/fully divine Messiah, there is no God-man atonement. Matthew, Mark and Luke all tell the birth of Christ from a different viewpoint. Matthew chronicles the birth from Jesus' genealogy, descending from Abraham and King David. Matthew is written towards a Jewish audience, capitalizing on the Scriptures that show Jesus as fulfillment of the Messiah teachings.

Luke tells the birth of Jesus Christ from the perspective of Mary and Joseph, their trip to Nazareth, and the stories of Jesus' childhood. Luke is written for the Christian community, struggling to form its identity and doctrine. The Gospel of Luke is about God's validation of Jesus as the Son of God. It's to the gospel of Luke that we owe our detailed knowledge of the birth of Christ. Luke was an educated Gentile and a physician, and a companion to Paul whose evangelism would bring the new faith into the broader world of non-Jews. Luke relates the story of the Roman-ordered census which requires households to register in the ancestral home of their family. Joseph of the lineage of David must register in Bethlehem. Mary, pregnant by the Holy Spirit, and Joseph travel to obey the law; while there, Mary gives birth to her son; there was no room in the town because of the census, and so they are lodged in a cave.

Matthew tells the story of how Herod, the King of the Jews and the puppet monarch of the Romans, learns that his kingdom will be supplanted by an infant who has been born. He sends Eastern astrologers or magi to find the infant. Herod says he plans to worship the baby, but the astrologers, also known as the wise men, after bringing the baby gifts head off in another direction so that they will not have to reveal the baby's whereabouts to the scheming king. Herod orders all infant males under the age of 2 to be murdered, ridding himself, he believes, of the problem of an inconvenient usurper to his thrown.

Mark tells the story of Jesus' ministry as a young adult. The primary importance of Mark is that Matthew and Luke both quote and rewrite portions of Mark to tell their stories. Mark is considered the oldest and most accurate of the four Gospels.

Jesus' Baptism by John the Baptist

Mark's gospel is the earliest one, assumed to be written sometime in the late 60s AD. Mark's gospel is the one scholars go to for reference. It is a straightforward, unadorned account of the ministry of Jesus that begins at the Jordan River, as the wild man prophet John the Baptist, identified in Luke as the cousin of Jesus, is preaching that the Messiah is coming and John is preparing the way. After John baptizes him, Jesus heads into the wilderness, a sort of spiritual boot camp for his ministry.

Jesus was baptized by John the Baptist, his cousin, in the Jordan River. The significance of His baptism is not for the remission of sin, as Jesus was sinless, but as a pattern for humanity to follow. At this baptism God announced from Heaven, "This is my Son, in whom I am well pleased." This was a public announcement from God of the divinity of Jesus Christ. This was also one of the few Scriptures that had the trinity in the same place at the same time, namely, God announcing from the heavens, Jesus being baptized in the river, and the Holy Spirit descending upon Jesus Christ "as a dove."

The Twelve Disciples

It would be easy to assume that, for the Jews of the ancient world, there were only a handful of numbers that had any real significance: the number 3, the number 7, the number 10, the number 12.

The number 12 is referred to in 187 places in the Bible. It's regarded as a perfect number that symbolizes the wholeness of the nation of Israel. Jacob had 12 sons, who headed the 12 tribes of Israel. Later, in the New Testament, when Jesus began his ministry, he chose 12 men to serve as his disciples.

The most famous of the 12 disciples was Simon Peter, the son of Jonas, a Galilean fisherman who lived in Bethsaida and Capernaum. His name in Hebrew, Cephas, meant rock and Jesus made a play on words when he told the impetuous, strong-willed fisherman that it was upon Cephas, this rock, that the church would be built. Peter was the acknowledged leader of the Twelve. He recognized that Jesus was the Son of God, an insight granted to him not by his own knowledge but by the revelation of God. But if Peter's conviction was clear, so were his sins and failings. The incident where he walks on water to meet Jesus until, looking down, he sees what he's doing and begins to fall into the water, shows how easily he—and all of us—can be weakened by doubt overruling faith, is indicative of his plight. Jesus warned him that on the night of Jesus' arrest, Peter would deny that he even knew the Lord. Peter insisted that such a thing would never happen, that he would always be faithful. But as the rooster crowed for the third time, Peter realized that Jesus' prediction had come true. But the memory of that failing stayed with him forever, imbuing his ministry with a courage born out of his determination not to fail Jesus a second time. Legend says that he requested to be crucified, when death was upon him, upside down because he did not deserve to die upright as Jesus had done. He may have denied his Lord once, but he proclaimed him for the rest of his life until his death.

Andrew was the brother of Simon Peter and it was Andrew who first introduced his brother to Jesus. Andrew was in search of a leader in the faith; before following Jesus, Andrew had been a disciple of John the Baptist. A fisherman by trade, evangelism was in his blood as he brought others to Jesus. When Jesus was preaching to the crowd of 5,000 people and realized that they were hungry, it was Andrew who observed that there was a boy who had brought some food—five loaves and two fishes---with him. That meal would turn into a miracle as Jesus fed the crowd with two fish and five small loaves of bread. When he left Jerusalem to bring the gospel of Jesus to others, he went to

Greece, although he is also honored as the patron saint of Russia and Scotland as well. He met his death in Greece after healing the governor's wife; she became a Christian, as did her husband. The governor's brother had Andrew arrested. Like Peter, Andrew regarded Jesus' death on the cross as too sacred for him to copy. So he, legend says, was crucified on a cross shaped like the letter X, now known as St. Andrew's cross.

James and John

John, the beloved disciple, managed to escape martyrdom, although in his later years, he spent years in exile on the island Patmos. He and his brother James, also a disciple, were ambitious in their early years as disciples and their mother was ambitious for them, asking Jesus to place her sons upon his right and left when he claimed his heavenly kingdom. The brothers were nicknamed the Sons of Thunder by Jesus. John's preaching took him to Asia Minor to spread the gospel, and the Bible includes his writings in I, II, and III John, Revelation, and perhaps the gospel of John.

His elder brother James was the first of the disciples to become a martyr for his faith in 44 AD when he was beheaded by King Herod.

Philip

Like Peter and Andrew, Philip was probably a fisherman. Philip was among the first to be called as a disciple by Jesus. He is mentioned in the miracle of the fishes and the loaves when he expresses the realistic observation that it would take over half a year's wages to buy enough bread for each of the 5,000 in the crowd to have a bite. After Jesus' ascension to heaven, Philip's preaching took him from Jerusalem, although scholars are not sure whether he was one of the seven ordained to be deacons mentioned in Acts. If the Apostle is also the Deacon, he is known for the story in which he explains the teachings of Jesus to the Ethiopian eunuch. Also convinced of his unworthiness, he accepted his martyrdom by hanging but said that his body should be wrapped in papyrus rather than linen because he was not worthy to be buried as Jesus has been buried.

Nathaniel

Like the brothers Andrew and Peter, Nathaniel, also called Bartholomew, was from Galilee. After Philip was called by Jesus to follow him, the enthusiastic new disciple went to Nathaniel with the news that the Messiah spoken of by Moses had been found, and he came from Nazareth. Nathaniel, apparently a skeptic, asked Philip whether anything good could come out of Nazareth. But he went with his friend, and when Jesus saw him, he said, "Behold, an Israelite indeed, in whom there is no guile." Nathaniel was stunned to hear that he was known to Jesus and he asked him, "How do you know me?" Jesus answered, "Before Philp called you, when you were under the fig tree, I saw you." Somehow, that clinched it for Nathaniel. He declared the rabbi from Nazareth to be the Son of God. Jesus sounded amused, asking Nathaniel if he believed this simply because Jesus told him he saw him under the fig tree? Jesus then promised Nathaniel that he would see much greater things than that; he would see the angels of God descending from the heavens upon the Son of God. Like the other disciples, Nathaniel traveled to other countries to preach the gospel, and is claimed by the Armenian Church as its patron saint. It's believed that he preached in India, and was martyred there, meeting his death by being flayed alive with knives.

Matthew or Levi

The call to discipleship which Jesus extended to Matthew the tax collector was life-changing for the man who was despised by the people of his community, but it shocked the citizens. Tax collectors who supported the Roman presence in an official capacity were despised, particularly if they were Jews who neglected the intrinsic teachings of their own faith to collaborate with the occupying force that had robbed the Jewish people of their political freedom. Jesus' penchant for accepting the hospitality of the outcasts made him a target for Jewish authorities and a mystery to the ordinary men and women who were taught that a holy, righteous man of God did not associate with sinners. Yet here was Jesus, the talk of the town, preaching, praying, healing, and doing miracles, and he was eating with the sinners. In their homes! And when chastised for his behavior, he turned the tables and accused the Pharisees and Sadducees of being hypocrites. Jesus simply went up to the tax collector and said, "Follow me." And Matthew did! Jesus didn't choose Matthew because it was the politically correct thing to do. He saw something in Matthew's heart that was waiting for a signal. Unlike the blue collar disciples who were fishermen, Mathew was a white collar guy. We can only wonder how Matthew managed to find his niche as a disciple. Tradition holds that he was a martyr but details of his death are not conclusive.

Thomas Didymus

Thomas, a Galilean, would travel far to spread the faith, finding martyrdom at the end of a spear in India. By then he had gotten over his doubts; this famous skeptic was not present when Jesus first appeared to his disciples following his resurrection. Thomas said that he would not believe the Lord had risen unless he saw for himself the imprints of the nails in Jesus' body. But when Jesus appeared to him, and allowed Thomas to satisfy his doubts, Thomas accepted the evidence and proclaimed Jesus as his Lord and his God.

James or James the Just
The identity of James depends on whether one believes that he is the son of Mary and therefore the brother of Jesus, or James, the son of Alphaeus. Because of the Roman Catholic belief that Mary's virginity continued throughout her marriage to Joseph, Catholic doctrine does not believe that Jesus had brothers or sisters born of Mary. In any case, James shared authority in Jerusalem with Peter. After Peter left the city. James became the Bishop of Jerusalem. Paul, the Apostle to the Gentiles, who never met Jesus, did meet James, said that he was encouraged by James to remember the poor when he preached. Because James was known to have entered the Holy of Holies in the Temple, a site forbidden to anyone but the High Priest, it's believed that Jesus' brother occupied this priestly role. Despite the authority of this position, James also met his death as a martyr, stoned by the Pharisees and the scribes.

Simon the Zealot
The Palestine of Jesus' time seethed with resentment against the occupation of the Romans, and not all malcontents were content merely with grumbling. The Zealots supported revolt against the Roman Empire, its governor, its legions, and all its representatives. According to the first century historian Josephus, the Zealots were reckless in both their good deeds and in their rebellion. Simon died a martyr to the Christian faith; according to tradition, he was crucified. Legend says that he was sawed to death in Persia, which is now the country of Iran. Other traditions

claim that his crucifixion took place in Samaria.

Thaddeus
This disciple is referred to as Jude in the gospel of Luke, but he's Thaddeus in Matthew and Mark. Naming of the disciples is not always consistent, creating some uncertainty among scholars. He preached in Assyria and Persia, and it was in the latter country that he was martyred, killed with arrows.

Judas Iscariot
Although Matthew might have had financial acumen, it was Judas who was the treasurer for the group. He was not from Galilee like the rest of the disciples; he was a Judean. The gospels accuse him of using his position as treasurer to steal from the purse. He is forever identified with 30 pieces of silver, the amount he was given in exchange for revealing where Jesus would be After informing the authorities that Jesus would be in the Garden of Gethsemane, Judas was overcome by remorse when Jesus was arrested, and he hanged himself.

Matthias, the 13th disciple
The disciples were well aware that Jesus intended for them to continue his work when he was no longer physically present. After the betrayal by Judas, and the guilt-stricken disciple's suicide, the disciples had to choose someone to fill his place so that they would again be twelve. There were two candidates: one named Joseph or Barsabas Justus, and one named Matthias. With the guidance of prayer, "You, O lord, who know the hearts of all, show which of these two You have chosen to take part in this ministry and apostleship from which Judas by transgression fell, that he might go to his own place." Prayer and the casting of lots selected Matthias as the replacement. There isn't much biographical

information on Matthias despite identifying him as one who had been with Jesus from the time that Jesus was baptized until his resurrection. Some historical sources say that Matthias, who preached along the Caspian and Cappadocian shores, lived until the year 80 AD.

The Sermon on the Mount

Jesus spent three years preaching to crowds. The sermon for which he is best known is called the Sermon on the Mount. Great crowds came to hear him and when Jesus saw the number of people, he went up on a mountain, his disciples around him. If the essence of Christianity were distilled into a single passage, it would be this signature sermon which took place early in Jesus' ministry, after he was baptized in the Jordan by John the Baptist.

Central to the sermon are the Beatitudes, where Jesus promises blessings to the poor in spirit, the mourners, the meek, the ones who hunger and thirst for righteousness, the merciful, the pure in heart, the peacemakers, the persecuted. Jesus promises that God will reward them for what they have endured.

The Gospel of Luke follows the blessings to those who suffer with woe to those who are rich, well fed, who laugh, and are well thought of. They have already received their rewards and will have to pay for them.

The path that Jesus describes is not an easy one. His definition of compassion to others shows that the followers of Jesus are expected to demonstrate love to the highest power: turn the other cheek; go the extra mile; if someone takes your shirt, give him your coat. How can anyone possibly do these things? By heeding the greatest commandments: Love the Lord your God with all your heart, with all your soul, with all your mind, with all your strength, and love your neighbor as much as you love yourself. Jesus explains, "All the law and the prophets hang on these two commandments."

Jesus said that he did not come to change the law. Instead, he liberated it. The law that had put a stranglehold on the advancement of the Jewish faith was liberated by the love of Jesus Christ. The strict interpretation of the law, which would not allow a man to be healed on the Sabbath and isolated the outcasts, was given an infusion of compassion by the Son of Man.

The Miracles of Jesus

The miracles that Jesus performed were an integral part of his ministry. For many in the crowd, the miracles were probably a form of entertainment, but they also served as convincing proof that this man from Nazareth was able to do things which no other human being could do. The miracles are categorized as miracles showing control over nature; raising the dead; casting out demons; and physical healings

Perhaps what is most intriguing about the miracles is not the ones he performed, but the ones he didn't. When he went home to Nazareth, it wasn't as the conquering hero. His former neighbors were impressed by his learning but disdainful of his background. Because of their lack of faith, he was unable to perform many miracles in Nazareth, an indication that Jesus' power calls upon the faith of the person requesting the miracle in order for the power to take effect. We see proof that faith is indeed very potent if it can be matched up with the right source.

Miracles of Nature

The first miracle which Jesus performed was not planned. Jesus was merely a guest, along with his mother Mary, at a local wedding in Cana. The family was running low on wine, a disgrace for a wedding, and Mary told her son, who said that it wasn't yet his time. But Mary moved forward, telling the household servants to do whatever Jesus told them to do. It may not have been his time, but he acted anyway, telling the servants to fill the vessels with water. When the guests drank it, they marveled that the host had saved the best wine for last.

When Jesus was preparing to call his disciples, he noticed that a trio of fishermen was not having any luck. He told them to try again, but this time, to head out into the deep water. Peter, James, and John had been working while Jesus preached, so they knew who he was. Peter agreed to do as Jesus asked, although he said that they had been fishing all night and had caught nothing. When they did what Jesus told them to do, their nets were so heavy with fish that they were breaking. Peter, realizing that this was not a coincidence, fell to his feet and begged Jesus to go away. But Jesus told him that from now on, he would be catching people instead of men.

Jesus attracted large crowds who came to hear him preach. When he realized that a crowd of 5000 needed to eat, he took five loaves of bread and two fish provided by a young boy who had had the foresight to bring a lunch with him. He blessed the food, and prayed to God. The lunch for a boy turned into more than enough food to feed 5000 people.

After feeding the crowd, Jesus needed time alone for prayer and he sent his disciples to go to the other side of the Sea of Galilee.

Darkness came and a storm arose, something which was a common occurrence. The disciples rowed fiercely to get out of the storm, and were startled to see a figure walking toward them. They thought they were watching a spirit but then they realized that it was Jesus, walking on top of the water. Peter began to walk toward Jesus but when he realized what he was doing, he began to sink into the water until Jesus helped him to safety.

Jesus was fast asleep in a boat with his disciples when a storm arose on the Sea of Galilee. The waves were breaking on the boat and the disciples feared that they would drown. They woke him up, perhaps a little irked that he was able to sleep while they tried to steer the boat in a storm. Jesus awoke and scolded the waves for their actions. He asked the disciples why they were frightened. "Do you still have no faith?" From relief at the rescue, the disciples were frightened anew at the realization that they were led by a man who could scold the wind and waves for their disobedience, and make them behave.

Miracles of Healing

We know that not all of the miracles of healing that Jesus performed were recorded in the gospel accounts because there were so many.

Leprosy was a dreaded disease in the ancient world. Lepers had to live outside the city where they would not be in contact with others. A leper came up to Jesus and begged him for a cure, telling Jesus that if he was willing, he could cleanse the man of leprosy. Jesus replied that he was willing and he touched the leper, who was immediately cured. Jesus instructed the former leper to show himself to the priest so that he could be pronounced clean and once again join human society, but he told him not to tell anyone what Jesus had done. However, the man was so overwhelmed by his cure that he told everyone he met. The news spread fast, which meant that Jesus had to keep a low profile, keeping to less populated areas rather than the center of the towns.

Jesus was on his way to the home of one Jairus, a man of importance in the synagogue, whose daughter was deathly ill, when he realized that someone had touched his cloak. He asked who had touched him. Trembling, a woman came forward and confessed that she was the one; she had touched his cloak because she had been bleeding for 12 years. That malady made her ritually unclean, but Jesus was not offended by what was a daring act. Instead, he told her, "Daughter, your faith has made you well."

Illness was seen as proof that someone had sinned. When Jesus came upon a man who had blind since he was born, the disciples asked him whether it was the man, or his parents, who had sinned. Neither had sinned, Jesus answered. Spitting on the ground, Jesus made mud and put the mud on the man's eyes. He told him to go and wash in the Pool of Siloam. His neighbors were astounded that the former beggar had regained his sight and they wanted to know what had happened. The man didn't know where Jesus had gone; he didn't know how his sight had returned. All he knew was that Jesus had cured his blindness.

Jewish society was rigidly organized. A faithful Jew avoided contact with lepers, Gentiles, and certainly the Romans. But when a Roman centurion went to Jesus on behalf of his servant, who was gravely ill, Jesus was prepared to go where he was needed. The centurion told him that he did not need to enter his home.

Because he was a leader of men, he knew that he had merely to give an order and it would be done. He understood that Jesus simply had to order that the servant should be healed and it would happen. Jesus was astounded; never, he said, had he witnessed such faith.

Some healings brought controversy. When Jesus went into a synagogue on the Sabbath, a day when no work was to be done, conventional wisdom was that he should have checked the miracles at the door. But Jesus saw a man with a withered hand and he healed him. His reason: was it better to do a good deed on the Sabbath, or to leave the man to his suffering? The Pharisees were outraged by what they regarded as a blasphemous attitude that, in their eyes, defied their laws. According to the Gospel of Mark, this act was what drove the Pharisees to plot against Jesus' life.

Casting out Demons

In Jesus' time, mental illness was explained as demon possession. Jesus exorcised many demons during his ministry, freeing the afflicted from the demons that ruled them. One of the most fascinating healings came about when a Canaanite woman, a Gentile, begged Jesus to heal her daughter, who was possessed. She was noisy and attracting attention and the disciples told Jesus to send her away. Jesus told the woman that he had not come to her but for the lost sheep of Israel. But she would not be dissuaded, and when he said that it was not right to take the bread that was for the children and instead throw it to the dogs, she retorted that even that dogs were allowed to eat the crumbs from the master's table. Jesus praised her faith and told her that her daughter was healed.

In the territory of the Gerasenes, there as a possessed man whose strength was so powerful that he broke the chains that bound him. Jesus went into the territory and ordered the demon to leave. The demon recognized Jesus, and begged him not to torment him. Jesus asked the demon his name and was told, "Legion, for we are many." The demons requests Jesus to send them into the herd of pigs; Jesus does so, and the herd of pigs hurl themselves down the hillside and into the lake, where they drown. The man, released from possession, is sane once more.

Raising the Dead

Healing the blind, the lame, the possessed could perhaps be explained. Walking on water and turning water into wine could be dismissed by skeptics as parlor tricks. But raising the dead?

Jesus was the master of life and death was not a challenge to him. So when he was en route to the home of Jairus to heal his dying daughter and a woman interrupted him because she needed healing, he paused to take the time to acknowledge her. A messenger came to tell him that he was no longer needed because the child had died. But Jesus ignored the suggestion and continued on his way. When he arrived, he told the assembled mourners that Jairus' daughter was asleep, not dead. He went upstairs accompanied by Jairus and his wife, Peter, James, and John. Jesus took the dead girl's hand and told her to get up. Returned to life, she opened her eyes and got up. In the midst of the mystery, Jesus was practical. He told her parents to give her food to eat. He also told them not to tell people what had taken place, to preserve his claim that she had been sleeping, not dead.

Jesus made a number of friends during his years in ministry and among his closest were Mary, Martha and Lazarus of Bethany. But when he learns that Lazarus is very ill, instead of hurrying to Bethany, he deliberately delays his arrival. When he finally gets there, Lazarus has been in the tomb for four days. Martha is angry at Jesus, telling him, "If you had been here, my brother would not have died." Jesus reminds her that whoever believes in him will live, even though he dies, and Martha affirms her belief that Jesus is the Messiah. Mary's grief moves him; he asks where Jesus is buried, and he weeps. When he orders the mourners to remove the stone in front of the tomb, Mary objects. Lazarus has been dead four days; there will be a terrible odor. But Jesus insists, and the stone is taken away. After praying, Jesus calls out, "Lazarus, come forth"

From the dark tomb comes Lazarus, still wrapped in the strips of linen with which the dead were buried. Lazarus is alive, and Jesus has taken the steps to his death. This miracle, more than any of the others, identified Jesus as a threat. When Jesus heads into Jerusalem to celebrate the Passover, he is hailed by the crowds who are aware of what happened and realize that he is no ordinary teacher. The Sanhedrin begin to plot how they can have Jesus put to death.

A man who travels the countryside of a small region bringing sight to the blind, mobility to the lame, food to the hungry, sanity to the mentally afflicted, and life to the dead is going to get attention. For the Jewish authorities, whose mission was to keep their community safely anchored in their ancestral land, the fear was that Jesus and his followers would stir up dissension which could cause the Romans to act. For the Jews, an oppressed people living in an occupied land, the need to maintain order was paramount. Even when they decided that Jesus must die, their reasoning was that it was better to kill one man for the common good. As the followers become more visible, the Jews came to regard them as a growing problem which required a definitive solution if the Hebrew people were to be safe.

The Last Supper in the Upper Room

In the last year of Jesus' ministry, fresh from the miracle of bringing Lazarus back to life, he goes to Jerusalem to observe the Passover. Jesus enters the Holy City triumphantly as the people welcome him with palm branches, the traditional welcome given to a king. He instructs the disciples to meet him in the Upper Room for the Passover meal. At this time Jesus announces that one of the disciples will betray him, knowing that the treasurer, Judas, has already done so by giving information about Jesus' location to the Jewish authorities. Jesus is arrested in the Garden of Gethsemane after Jesus and his disciples had celebrated the Passover. Judas had told the authorities that the man he would kiss would be the one they sought. This act, committed with a gesture usually reserved as a token of affection has forever branded Judas as the ultimate betrayer.

The Crucifixion and Resurrection

Jesus is taken before the Roman governor Pilate, who has him flogged but could discern no evidence that any crime had been committed. In fact, Pilate seems intrigued by the silent man brought to him for punishment. Because he is a Jew, Jesus is sent to Herod Antipas, but Herod returns him to Pilate. Pilate is not eager to pronounce sentence upon this person who seemed innocent of wrongdoing and will offer no word in his own defense, but Pilate, like the Jews, wanted to avoid anything which could attract the attention of the Romans. Jesus is sentenced to death. Jesus carries the wooden beam which would be affixed to his place of execution at Calvary. He is nailed to the cross, which after his death comes to be regarded not as a symbol of execution but as the imprint of his sacrifice for the people who believe. With the words, "It is finished," Jesus dies. His disciples, except for John, had fled in fear; in fact Peter had denied even knowing Jesus when he was confronted by residents of the city who recognized him. Jesus is placed in a tomb that belonged to Joseph of Arimathea, a Pharisee who believed in his ministry. The stone is rolled in front of the tomb, and the authorities place guards there so that no one could claim the body and attribute the resurrection which Jesus had foretold.

When Mary, one of his devoted followers, arrives at the tomb three days after his death, she finds the stone rolled away, the guards absent, and a young man that she takes to be the gardener the only one there. Until the gardener calls her by name, she doesn't recognize the risen Christ as the teacher she had followed. The disciples, when Mary tells them the story, are dubious until Jesus appears in their midst where they are hiding in the upper room.

Throughout the three years that he spends with the disciples in ministry, preparing them for the time when he will no longer be with them, Jesus let his disciples know that he will be put to death. But he reassures them that he will rise again. His disciples reply, we know you will rise again but Jesus means in three days' time after his crucifixion. The concept of resurrection was a challenging one for the disciples, who despite all that they had witnessed during his ministry, were still ordinary men who grieved for the loss of their teacher, leader, and friend. When Jesus' tomb is opened after three days, they learn that, just as he promised, he is no longer there for he has risen! The raising of Christ into the heavens is just the beginning; what God has raised once, God will raise again. Those who believe in Christ will be raised up into heaven also. This is the most important story in Christianity as, without the death and resurrection of Jesus, there is no salvation for humanity. Jesus serves as the perfect sacrifice, as He is without sin, unlike any other human being. With his death and resurrection, we are able to enter the Kingdom of God.

Later, in the Book of Acts, also believed to be written by Luke, the disciples come out of hiding on the Day of Pentecost, regarded as the birthdate of the Christian Church. Peter, no longer afraid, boldly preaches to a crowd of people who, although they are from different lands and speak different languages, all understand what he is saying. A mighty wind and tongues of fire accompany the unleashing of the Holy Spirit and the disciples, emboldened by its power, are moved to preach the gospel of Jesus.

The Great Commission

Jesus commands the disciples to go to the ends of the earth, baptizing in the name of the Father, the Son, and the Holy Spirit. Jesus promises to be with mankind, even unto the ends of the earth. The significance of this passage for Christians is that each person must also preach and teach and baptize, following the Great Commission, spreading the Good News of Jesus' saving work to all unbelievers.

When Jesus left his disciples, he told them to go and make disciples of all nations. But 'the early ministry of the new faith was focused on preaching to the Jews, which was understandable, since Christianity's roots were firmly in Judaism. The early church was loving, self-sacrificing, and supportive of one another even through persecution. Peter, Jesus' disciple, and James, Jesus' brother, were the leaders of the Jerusalem-based religion. The disciples did travel to spread the gospel, but under their leadership the Church remained a sect of the larger Jewish tradition. What no one realized was that a formidable new ally, formerly a foe, with a penchant for writing letters, was about to transform a small sect into a global religion.

The Teachings of Jesus

The gospel of John is written near the end of the first century AD, the last of the gospels to be recorded. While the first three gospels are regarded as having historical authenticity, scholars are undecided about the authenticity of John; this gospel may have had multiple sources. Its late date may reflect the mounting tensions between established Judaism and burgeoning Christianity.

Taken collectively, however, the gospels provide the foundation for modern knowledge of the ministry of Jesus. He traveled throughout Judea for approximately three years, healing the sick, teaching, preaching, performing miracles and instructing his followers to practice forgiveness and to welcome the outcast. He comes into conflict with the Jewish authorities when he appears to disregard the strict laws which the Pharisees practiced. But Jesus said that he did not come to change the Law of Moses. However, he gave two Old Testament commands a new emphasis. The greatest commandment, Jesus said, is to love the Lord your God with all your heart, soul, mind, and strength, which is taken from Deuteronomy. The second commandment comes from Leviticus: You shall love your neighbor as yourself. If Christianity were to be distilled down to its most basic essence, it would be these two commandments.

Paul the Apostle to the Gentiles

The early Christians met in one another's homes, often covertly because their worship was forbidden. The Greek word ichthys is an acrostic for Jesus Christ, God's Son Savior. The legend holds that one Christian would draw the initial lines of a fish in the sand to determine whether he was in the company of believers. Another Christian would finish the drawing by forming the missing semicircle. The symbol worked as a private means of identification because Jesus Christ was strongly identified with fishermen; several of them, notably Peter, James and John, made their living by fishing in the Sea of Galilee. They were at their trade when the Nazareth preacher told them to sail out into the deep water and throw down their nets. Peter obeyed, despite his doubts. The nets were so filled with fish that they began to break, and Peter realized that he was in the presence of no ordinary man. Jesus called them to catch men and women instead of fish and the three followed him. From the deep waters of the Galilee to the depths of the human condition, the disciples found an audience for their promise of hope to those who believed in Jesus Christ. Despite the danger, they continued to spread the gospel.

A devout Jew named Saul, from Tarsus, proved relentless in his search for Christians to turn over to the authorities. He was present at the stoning of Stephen, the first Christian martyr. Stephen's death begins a period of persecution for the Jerusalem Christians, and Saul of Tarsus was one of the primary oppressors of the followers of Christ who, he was convinced, preached heresy against the Jewish beliefs. One day, when he is on his way to Damascus, he is struck blind by God. He is cared for by a Christian named Ananias. Saul regains his sight, is renamed Paul, and becomes as zealous in his evangelism for Christianity as he had been vigorous in its persecution. His perspective was different from that of the disciples who had worked intimately with Jesus. Paul concedes that they had worked directly with the Lord he now served, but he refuses to believe that their message is superior to his. Hard-headed, energetic Paul and the Jerusalem leaders are destined to butt heads.

The issue of what to do about Gentiles who wanted to convert to Christianity had not quite been resolved. They are welcome to do so, but with the understanding that they need to become Jews first, obeying Jewish traditions which required circumcision. Writing to the Galatian church, Paul explains that it's faith, not previous tradition, which binds a believer to Jesus. Paul believes this was unnecessary; in his letter to the members of the church at Colossae, he reinforces his belief that circumcision is unnecessary because in Christ, a person is made new. Faith, not works, justifies salvation.

Paul was an energetic traveler on behalf of the Christian church. His travels to other cities established centers of the faith in those areas which were beyond the circle of the Jerusalem-based church, and if James and Peter minister to the Jews, Paul reaches out to the Gentiles.

It's safe to say that, had Paul been a reluctant traveler and an irregular correspondent, the Christian Church would have evolved into a very different entity. But the man who endured shipwrecks, pirates, and dissension from his colleagues was not going to be stopped.

When word reaches the Jerusalem Church that great things were happening in Antioch, a Christian leader named Barnabas fetches Paul and together they go to Antioch, spending a year preaching and teaching. It's at the Antioch church that the followers of the offshoot of Judaism are first referred to as the Christians. The struggles between the Jewish and Christian factions continue, frequently leading to violence. But as the missionaries travel, they choose elders who can lead the church in their absence.

As Paul travels, he develops strong bonds with the new converts. When he travels to Corinth, he meets fellow tentmakers Aquila and his wife Priscilla. He stays there for a time and when he leaves, Priscilla and Aquila go with him.

His visit to Ephesus is the occasion for a riot as the local craftsmen demonstrate their concern that Paul's success with converting pagans who purchased idols in silver would lead to a loss of business. The mob is quieted by an Ephesian clerk who urges them to be calm; if the craftsmen had a grievance, they should press charges through the courts. After the account of Paul raising Eutychus from the dead in Troas, the Book of Acts suddenly switches from the third person narrative to first person. Scholars are not united on the narrator who uses the pronoun "we" to continue the story of the early church, but feel that it must have been an eyewitness to the events which took place.

Paul decides to return to Jerusalem, a decision which arouses fears for his safety from his friends, but Paul is insistent and initially, it goes well. He tells the leaders of the success among the Gentiles. But a riot breaks out, which brings the attention of the Roman authorities, who arrest Paul. But when Paul tells the centurion that he is a Roman citizen, Paul's chains are removed.

The Roman commander is puzzled by what happened, and arranges to have Paul speak before the chief priests and the ruling Sanhedrin. Paul establishes his credentials as a devout Jew and a Pharisee. But his efforts are in vain.

The Roman commander fears for Paul's life and brings him back to the barracks for his own safety. A plot to kill Paul forms, and the Romans transfer Paul to Caesarea. Paul is tried by Felix the governor; the Jewish elders who testify describe Paul as a ringleader of what they called the Nazarene sect. Paul testifies in his defense. Felix meets with him frequently, but leaves him in prison. The new governor, Festus, hears the testimony of the Jewish leaders against Paul. Paul defends himself, asserting that he had not violated Jewish law, the Jewish temple, or Caesar. As a Roman citizen, he has the right to appeal to Caesar and he does so.

The trip to Italy begins with poor weather and winds which blow the ship off course; the passengers are shipwrecked. When they seek refuge on the island of Malta, the passengers are well treated and Paul is appreciative of their kindness. When they depart Malta for Rome, they arrive safely. Paul lives in a rented house under Roman guard, and continues his preaching during his house arrest for two years. Tradition holds that he was executed by Emperor Nero during one of the rounds of persecution sometime in the mid-60s AD. His Roman citizenship would have spared him death by crucifixion; beheading would have been the means of execution.

With limited means of communication, the early church relied on letters to extend messages and encourage teaching with the new churches which formed after Jesus' death and resurrection. Paul is renowned for his letters which form the backbone of Christian theology, but letters from other sources are also preserved in the New Testament. Paul tends to reap all the theological headlines for his letters to the churches he started, but the letters written by the other church leaders carried a great deal of weight as difficult questions were being asked.

The New Testament Epistles
It sometimes seems that, after the resurrection of Jesus, when the growth of the church was an earthly endeavor, there's Paul and everyone else. That's not quite true. The early church fathers (and mothers, although they have not been credited with authorship of the books included in the Bible) brought their own unique perspectives to their ministry, as well as their memories or understanding of Jesus. The early church was wrestling with its identity, just as the early Jewish followers had to discern who they were after they left Egypt.

The Book of Hebrews, once attributed to Paul, is now regarded as the work of an unknown author, although it may have been written by one of the believers who traveled with Paul.

The letters written by James are a minor mystery; it's believed they were written by Jesus' brother because the other James of significance, the disciple and brother of John, was martyred in 44 AD. James focuses on developing faith through adversity. Through prayer and living as God wishes, believers can overcome hardship. James is famous for the verse, "Faith without works is dead," which affirms the need to conduct one's life in a manner that lives out the faith that believers profess.

Peter is the disciple who was chosen by Jesus to leave his life as a fisherman and fish for believers. Shaken by his failure to support Jesus at the time of the crucifixion, Peter's courage is reborn at Pentecost and he flings himself into the role that Jesus predicted for him. Peter's authorship of the epistles bearing his name came under scrutiny because of the belief that an unlettered fisherman could not have written the letters. But supporters remind us that, although Peter did not have a rabbinical background, there's no indication that he was illiterate. The world in which he preached was one of more than one language and, empowered by the Holy Spirit, Peter was transformed in his ministry. Peter's encouragement of believers to maintain their faith in persecution would have a personal bent, as it's believed that Peter was executed by Nero around the same time as Paul, in the early-to-mid 60s AD. Suffering, Peter writes, is temporary; believers will be delivered. Peter is regarded as the first pope of the Christian Church, the "rock" as Jesus phrased it, upon whom he would built his church. Peter, also living in a time of turmoil, emphasizes that believers need to concentrate on the message of God and not be distracted. He can write with credibility of the need to keep the faith because he had also suffered for his believes. Knowing that martyrdom was inevitable given his visibility as a leader of the Christians, Peter wanted to make sure that the young flock received comfort during the years of persecution.

John's letters, also credited to the disciple, indicate a close familiarity with Jesus. The early church was prey to impersonators and false teachers. John, echoing a warning from Peter, instructs his readers to be on their guard. The dating of the letters indicates that they were written in the late 80s AD, before Domitian began his persecution in 95 AD.

Jude is believed to have been written by another of Jesus' brothers. Jude urges his readers to be steadfast in the faith and faithful to God, but wary of false teachings.

James and Jude are half-brothers to Jesus, born to Mary and Joseph. While little is known of the childhood of Jesus, we can assume that he grew up in a household dedicated to observation of Jewish principles and kindness. His brothers followed him in ministry. According to sources, James was sentenced by the Sanhedrin to death by stoning in the early 60s AD. Legend says that Jude was martyred during the reign of the Emperor Trajan, who ruled Rome from 98-117 AD.

Perhaps no book of the Bible has been discussed, interpreted, and analyzed more than Revelation. It's the basis for the popular Christian fiction *Left Behind* series written by Tim LeHaye and Jerry B. Jenkins. It's a point of reference for every political leader who is assumed to be the Antichrist du jour; most recently, Saddam Hussein and Mikhail Gorbachev were identified as the Antichrist. But this last book of the New Testament is regarded as a book of prophecy with a purpose directly related to the members of the early Christian church.

Dated near the end of the first century AD, the Book of Revelation is the work of a Christian known as John the Elder, written to the seven Asian churches while the writer was on the island of Patmos. It was probably not written by John the disciple. Apocalyptic literature was, in a way, a form of code for readers who already had the inside scoop on what was going on; what to us is encrypted was revealed to them. Angels, trumpets, scrolls, signs, seals, the 144,000 who are saved, the Beast and his mark, 666, war between God and Satan, the battle of Armageddon—the

Apocalypse has become a modern cottage industry in conspiracy theory. But for the Christians of this time who faced persecution for their beliefs, Revelation was a promise that God would ultimately triumph over Rome, the Great Whore of Babylon and the Beast, the Roman emperor.

Chapter 4: Christology

Christology is the study of the nature and purpose of Jesus Christ as expressed in the Gospels and the letters of the New Testament. There are many forms of Christology throughout the world, but this work will identify the three most common and often evangelized within the United States.

1.   Atonement theory

The atonement theory is the understanding that Jesus Christ is the Son of God and the only source through which salvation is offered. Atonement can be broken down into at-one-ment, meaning that Jesus brings humanity and God into reconciliation, or at-one-ment in spirit.

Atonement theory has many branches, each one has a different meaning although the terms are often interchanged. One of the first understandings of how atonement works is through the moral influence theory. This theory was first popular in the 2nd and 3rd centuries, and again in the Middle Ages, and currently in the writings of Tillich and Kant. In the moral influence theory Christians are instruments of moral change, following the teachings of Jesus Christ. and his inclusion of the tax collectors and sinners.

The ransom theory of atonement is that Jesus has liberated humankind from the slavery of sin and death by giving his life as a ransom sacrifice. (Matthew 20:28) Victory over death and Satan is by giving Jesus life (perfect) in place of humankind (imperfect).

In the satisfaction theory, humankind owes a debt to God, not Satan. Jesus is the only acceptable sacrifice because Jesus is both God and man. In the satisfaction theory of atonement, Jesus gave himself as sacrifice for many to the One God. 1 Corinthians 15:22

Anselm's satisfaction theory extended, and popularized by the Reformers, is a type of penal substitution theory, as sin is considered the breaking of the moral law set in place by God. Utilizing Romans 3:23 (the wages of sin is death), penal substitution theory states that the breakers of the moral law are subject to the justice of God and God's wrath, and only the reparation by Jesus Christ's saving blood will redeem the sinner. Galatians 3:13. "Jesus became the curse for us."

2. Jesus as Exemplar

Jesus as exemplar is the christology that Jesus' actions and words teach us how to behave towards God and humankind. Through Jesus' self-sacrifice of crucifixion, Christians are taught to be self-sacrificing. The crucifixion compels the Christian to both act like Jesus and be like Jesus, emptying ourselves of our selfish nature to take on the nature of God and Christ. Abelard, the main proponent of Exemplar Christology, proposes that Christians follow the teachings of God out of love for God rather than fear of God. Those that love God will keep his commandments and love his neighbor as himself. God is seen not as a God of demands but as a God of beckoning love through the example that was shown in the life of Jesus Christ. 1 John 4:8 "God is love."

3.   Jesus the Liberator

Liberation theology is the understanding that Jesus is the friend of the poor, the oppressed, the sick and the wounded. Jesus as liberator confronts the oppressors, the rich, and the greedy to give up their riches and serve God. Christians that see Jesus as Liberator understand Jesus to be the example of a champion of the underdog and the downtrodden. As a Christian following the teachings of Jesus the Liberator, the servant (Christian) would be actively seeking to challenge the powers and principalities that perpetuate injustices in the world.

Chapter 5: Theology

What is theology? Theology is the study of the nature of God and the beliefs that are informed by this study.

There are many types of Christian Theology. The term theology was first used in Plato's discourse in the third century, B.C. Aristotle, likewise, discussed theology in his works, specifically discussing the nature of God, the Divine Source. In the later writings of Augustine and forward through the Middle Ages, the meaning of theology was interpreted to "a discussion of the nature and intent of God."

In current circles, from the 18th century and beyond, the study of theology is not limited to Christian teachings. There is also theology of Hinduism, a theology of Islam, and a theology of Judaism, for example.

There are common concepts of God within Christian theology. The four major divisions of Christianity are thus: Evangelical, Liberal, Fundamentalist, and Conservative, and are also divided into the Protestant and Roman Catholic sectors. All agree that God is omnipotent, omniscient, and omnipresent. God is also understood as both present in the world, and beyond the world, known as imminent and transcendent. Christianity within mainline theology also agrees that God is of the Trinity, existing as the Father, the Son, and the Holy Spirit, but also being One.

It may be difficult, in today's secular society, to understand the grip which theology had on Western civilization as Christianity became the dominant religious force. But the controversies that arose when Christians interpreted teachings and Scripture differently were regarded as heresy, and heretics were punished severely for their views. Kings were believed to rule by divine right; therefore, the purity of the nation's religious observation was a matter of political, as well as religious, significance. Christians are no longer condemned to burn at the stake for unorthodox views, and the passage of time has secured the basic tenets of Christian belief.

1. There is one God, the Beginning and the End; Jesus taught believers to call God "Father."

2. Jesus is the Son of God, wholly divine and wholly human, who came to Earth to live as humans did in order to bring salvation to a people who were otherwise lost forever to sin. Jesus' death on the cross is the means by which sins are forgiven.

3. The Trinity is God, Jesus, and the Holy Spirit.

4. Justification by faith means that Christians who believe in Jesus Christ are blessed and forgiven by God.

5. The body will die, but believers who live a live according to God's teachings will live again.

6. Baptism is a sacrament which brings a believer into the faith.

   The Eucharist, or Holy Communion, commemorates the meal that Jesus shared with his disciples on the night that he was arrested and sentenced to die. The bread and the wine which symbolize the body and blood of Christ are eaten and drunk in memory of Jesus.

Chapter 6: Soteriology

Soteriology is the study of the doctrine of salvation; within Christianity it is the study of the saving work of Jesus Christ.

Within Christianity salvation is the saving of the soul through redemption, because of the taint of sin and its consequences. Salvation is obtained exclusively through Jesus Christ's life, death, and resurrection. Christian doctrine offers a wide range of soteriology, from exclusive salvation, meaning the saving of the soul from death and destruction because of sin's manifestations, to universalism, the soteriology that all human souls will be reconciled to God, because of God's unlimited love and mercy towards humankind.

Soteriology is generally accepted as the concept that all of humanity is made acceptable to God through the actions of Jesus Christ, His Son, and his death on the cross. Jesus said that unless a person was born again, he could not be saved. This concept befuddled his listeners; Nicodemus, a respect Pharisee who was not hostile to Jesus, asks how a person could re-enter the womb? But the rebirth that Jesus described was not gynecological. "If I have told you people about earthly things and you don' believe, how will you believe if I tell you about heavenly things?"

It is God's desire to save the world. In order to do that, it was necessary for God to send his son as a sacrifice so that salvation can take place. "For God did not send his Son into the world to condemn the world, but that the world should be saved through him."

Chapter 7: Pneumatology

Pneumatology is the study of the Biblical doctrine as regarding the Holy Spirit. Included in this study is the personhood of the Holy Spirit, the work of the Holy Spirit, and the deity of the Holy Spirit.

It is revealed in Scripture that the Holy Spirit is sent by Jesus as a comforter in John 14:16. The Holy Spirit teaches, makes choices, reveals Jesus, convicts, intercedes in prayer, can be lied to, can be grieved, and can be quenched, and can be resisted, all examples of personhood.

The work of the Holy Spirit is to inspire Scripture, rejuvenate hearts, create, sustain and give life to all things. The Holy Spirit is eternal and omniscient. The Holy Spirit, as part of the Trinitarian Godhead, is Divine.

The Holy Spirit is mentioned in both the Old and the New Testaments.

One of the interesting things that we learn as we explore the teachings of the Bible is that, although we understand our concept of God to include God the Father, God the Son, and God the Holy Spirit as it's outlined in the Apostles' Creed, the Bible itself does not refer to the Trinity. The term was first used near the end of the second century by early church scholar Tertullian and gained in prominence during the fourth and fifth centuries. This was one of the many issues which the famed Council of Nicea wrestled when it met in 325 at the behest of Constantine, the Roman emperor who converted to Christianity and found that establishing the theology of a new faith was just as demanding as his imperial duties. But the concept of the Holy Spirit, the third entity of the Trinity, as sharing the divinity of God and Jesus, was not affirmed until the Council of Constantinople in 381.

For some Christians, the Trinity remains a stumbling block. Even Cyril Richardson, as a professor of the Union Theological Seminary in New York, acknowledged that the Trinity is an artificial construct because its establishment as doctrine does not come to the faith via the Bible.

Yet we know that Jesus Christ himself affirmed the importance of the Holy Spirit to his disciples. He promised that when he was gone from his earthly life, he would not leave the disciples without comfort. He would sent them a Helper, a Counselor, an Advocate, the Spirit of Holiness, who would continue to teach the followers, reminding them of what Jesus had said. It is Jesus who establishes the significance of the Holy Spirit when he tells his disciples in Matthew 12:32 that anyone who speaks against the Son of Man will be forgiven, but not so those who speak against the Holy Spirit. The condemnation, Jesus warns, will follow from the current age into the age to come.

The Holy Spirit made its New Testament debut in a dramatic, unforgettable manner that was so powerful that it shaped a crowd of strangers into an improvised worship service that served as no less than the birthday of the Christian Church.

Fifty days after Easter, the disciples were still frightened by the political events that had sent Jesus to the cross. They were fortified by his resurrection and his reappearance into their lives, but when he was gone and they did not have his physical presence for comfort, they had to rely on his promise that he would send a Helper, the Holy Spirit, to help them. In fact, his promise said "Very truly, I tell you, the one who believes in me will also do the works that I do and, in fact, will do greater works than these . . ."

It was a momentous day, according to the Book of Acts. Present were the eleven disciples along with Matthias who had been chosen to replace Judas the betrayer, and numerous followers of Jesus, including his mother. They were still in the Upper Room, in Jerusalem, a city that was crowded with people from all over the region because they were celebrating the Hebrew festival of Shavuot, or the Festival of Weeks, which commemorates the giving of the Ten Commandments to Moses from God.

At nine o'clock in the morning, a mighty wind arose from heaven, and tongues of fire were seen above the heads of the apostles, the signature symbols of the Holy Spirit, which filled the crowd. Although the assembly included Medes, Mesopotamians, Judeans, Cappadocians, Pontusians, Asians, Pamphylians, Egyptians, Cyrenians, and Romans, Cretans, and Arabs, they were able to understand Peter when he began to preach. The crowd was naturally bewildered and amazed that with so many nations and languages represented, they were all able to understand. But Peter was not surprised. Nor was he drunk, which was the charge hurled at him by the incredulous crowd. The craven follower who denied Jesus when he was arrested was afire with the Holy Spirit and he plunged into preaching, beginning with the prediction of Joel that the day would come when God would pour out his Spirit, and continuing with the holy credentials of the Son of God. The Christian Church was born in splendor and mystery, awash in the Holy Spirit.

Chapter 8: Studying the Bible

By this point in this book, for a Christian disciple, it cannot be emphasized enough the importance of reading and studying the Bible. The Bible in its entirety as a reading from cover to cover may be overwhelming and even confusing to a new believer or one who has not often spent time with books. There are many approved and stimulating ways to study the Bible. Below we have listed just four effective ways.

1. Chapter by Chapter

Reading the Bible from Genesis to Revelation, chapter by chapter, is one way of understanding the entirety of the Word of God. When reading from cover to cover, try not to get bogged down in the genealogies or the "begats," as they are sometimes called. Instead look for the gist of the passage.

Keep a notebook handy if you choose to read the Bible by chapter. At the end of the chapter reading, write down a two or three sentence synopsis of your understanding of what happened in that chapter. Write down the key characters and the most important verse. Try to decipher the theme of the passage. Look for a repetition of ideas. List key words in the chapter like faith, or prayer, or desire.

If you read a passage that makes no sense to you, back up and read the preceding chapter again. See if there is a continuation of thought or actions. If that does not help your understanding, read forward a chapter.

There are 1,189 chapters in the Bible. If you wish to complete the Bible in one year, you will need to read approximately 3 chapters a day, or thirty minutes of Bible study.

Many who are making their way through the Bible find it effective to make notes by verses that strike a personal chord. Familiarity with Bible verses resonate with faith seekers. In times of trial, finding comfort in a favored verse can provide solace. Because the Bible is one of the most heartfelt of books that a believer can own, noting one's thoughts and responses to particular verses gives scripture a powerful personal meaning.

2. Read the Bible Topically

Pick one topic, for example, salvation, and search for every Scripture that addresses salvation. When using this method of Bible study, it is helpful to have a Strong's Exhaustive Concordance or a Thompson Chain Reference or Scofield edition of the Bible. These Bibles have additional features that link the passages of Scripture according to topic.

An online resource is Nave's Topical Study Tool. Developed by a Navy Chaplain, Nave's Topical Study tool covers 20,000+ topics and subtopics that are cross-referenced throughout the Scriptures. Nave's can be found at:

http://www.biblestudytools.com/concordances/naves-topical-bible/

3. Chronological Study of the Bible

Even though the Bible has the books listed in a specific and identical order in every Bible, these books are not placed in chronological order. Within this book I listed a chart of Old and New Testament Scriptures in their chronological order. It is interesting to note that some breaks are in the middle of some books instead of at the end. For example, the oldest scriptures in the Bible are Genesis chapters 1-10, then followed by Job 1-42, then back to Genesis. Reading the Bible in chronological order instead of cover to cover may help one to understand the historical passage of time in relationship. It will also help to visually see the battles and struggles of each character, as the passages flow more readily.

To complete this Bible reading in one year, you will need to read approximately 3 chapters a night.

4. By Character Name

Instead of reading the Bible from cover to cover, try reading the Bible by character name and event. In this manner, they are 3,237 people in the Bible. Unfortunately, some names are repeated so it can be difficult to ascertain who is affiliated or related to whom. It is best when studying by character name to keep a written note of whom you are studying, and make a small genealogy chart of the person's mother and father and relatives, if listed.

This will enable you to see the direction relationship between David and Jesse, for example, and Solomon. (son, father, and grandson, respectively) Not every character mentioned in the Bible is significant or has committed a great deed, but every character is known by God and that is important within itself.

92

If you decide to study the Bible by character, you will need a notebook to list each name and family affiliation. Beside each name you list note why you think they are mentioned in the Bible and what happens to this person. This information will give you a wide view of the mercy of God and the actions of God's people in crisis and in faith.

Chapter 9: Making a Study Plan

Many people desire to read and study the Bible but are waylaid by the busy actions of the day. Often the desire is overcome by exhaustion and running out of time.

If you want to really study the Word of God, you have to make time. First choose the amount of time you wish to be engaged in the study of the Bible. Be honest with yourself. Do you want to spend 15 minutes a day? Do you want to spend 30 minutes a day? How much of a priority do you want to make your Bible study?

Once you have honestly evaluated the time commitment you want to make, then look at your daily schedule. Where do you want to place God? First in the day, to open your eyes? or last in the day, to give you a peaceful heart? Maybe over your lunch break, to give a fresh look at the world and away from the troublesome business day?

Your next decision will be which method you will use to study. Do you like routine? Reading through the Bible cover to cover will appeal to you? Do you like things to be in the right order? Reading the Bible chronologically will appeal to your sense of symmetry. Do you like things to be mixed up and random? Reading the Bible by character name is often the solution to a reader that prefers changeability. If you like to do things one at a time, then reading topically will appeal to your sense of completeness.

Making Time for the Bible

Now that you have selected the method of Bible study, and the time commitment you want to make, look at your daily schedule and write in Bible Study. Make it a priority and you will find the personal time to accomplish feeding your spiritual hunger. As your soul is reaching for God, you need to saturate your mind and soul with the Word of God. You will find after three weeks the interference in your daily routine has now become a habit. You will now feel empty and out of sorts if you skip your daily time with the Word.

Accountability

Now that you have chosen your method, made your commitment to study, and scheduled your personal time in your private calendar, you need to find either a Study Buddy or a person to which you will be accountable. Saying that you want to study and actually fulfilling your commitment will be much easier when you have to report daily or weekly to another person about your promises.

Accountability is not about spying on another person, it is instead about helping the other person take control of their time and their spiritual life. You may choose to read the Bible together or separately, you may commit and contact by telephone, text, Facebook, or in person. The point is that a partner makes everything work together more smoothly.

Chapter 10: How to Memorize Scripture

Memorizing Scripture as a child is an easily accomplished task. Children's minds are like sponges, they absorb information with no need for memory prompts or mnemonic devices. A child's mind until the age of about 10 will absorb words and language quickly and with little effort. Their brain just expands to take in the new information and retain it.

An adult brain works differently. The adult brain, after the age of ten or so, needs a hook to continue to memorize. A hook is a memory device that helps your brain hold on to the information that is desirable to retain. You might be using a hook to remember someone's name, for example, by associating that person, Mr. Brown, with brown shoes. Each time you see Mr. Brown you may look at his shoes and remember him, or you may visualize his head in the shape of a shoe. This is a memory hook.

When memorizing the Bible you may need memory hooks, flash cards, or even index cards taped to your mirror or visor on your car. Any of these methods will help you to retain the Bible verses you desire.

You might ask, "Why do I want to memorize Scripture anyway? It sounds like a lot of hard work."

You are correct. It IS a lot of hard work and takes personal fortitude, perseverance and grit. It takes the willingness to push on through a hard situation in order to reap a greater benefit. What is the greater benefit?

Hiding the Word of God in your heart allows you to pull God's promises from your heart in times of need. You won't always have access to your cell phone, Kindle, or even your paper Bible. These are the times that holding God's truths in your heart will make your soul sing and your spirit soar.

Memorizing Scripture is absolutely the foundation for personal growth. When you memorize Scripture you fill your minds and thoughts with spiritual food. Think of how many songs you have memorized from the secular world. The words continue to play in your head in a continuous loop, affecting your thoughts and desires. Have you ever sung the "Oscar Meyer wiener song?" Did you eventually that day end up eating a hot dog, whereas before it was not even on your meal plan?

Filling your mind with Scripture will enhance your prayer life, strengthen your witness, improve your personal outlook and attitude, increase your confidence and self-esteem, and give you a rock solid faith.

The benefits of memorizing Scripture are as follows:

- It will make you more Christ-like. As you take on the Word of God, you also take on the Word, Christ. You will begin to think more about Godly things and less about earthly issues and conflicts.

- It will help you keep yourself free from sin. When sin tempts, having the Word of God on your heart and in your mind elevates your actions and words.

- It will help you defeat Satan. When Satan tries to overcome you, follow Jesus in quoting Scripture back to him.

- It will make you a more effective witness of the Gospel to unbelievers. When you witness and quote the essential truths to a non-believer, they are impressed that you care enough about your God to memorize His word.

- It will help you in your personal devotions with God. When you have a heart full of Scripture, you can shout to the heavens, "Make a joyful noise unto the Lord, all ye lands! Serve the Lord with gladness, come before His presence with singing! Know ye that the Lord He is God, it is He that hath made us and not we ourselves."

How many times have you seen a pompous fool shouting about being a self-made man? Remember that we are God's people, and the sheep of His pastures. Renewing our relationship with God through Scripture affirms our place in the Word, and in the World, grounded in and by our faith.

What Should I Memorize?

This is a question you may be asking yourself. There are so many important Scriptures, where might I begin? We turned to the website of Crosspointe Church for a list of 25 important Scriptures. Crosspointe Church offers the following Scriptures as a beginning for memorization. After these are memorized there are many sources that will offer more suggestions, including the Navigators.

https://www.navigators.org/Tools/Discipleship%20Resources/Tools/Topical%20Memory%20System

The Human Condition

For the wages of sin is death, but the free gift of God is eternal life in Christ Jesus our Lord. Romans 6:23

God Provides

And my God will meet all your needs according to his glorious riches in Christ Jesus. Philippians 4:19

God's Love

For God so loved the world, that he gave his only Son, that whoever believes in him should not perish but have eternal life. John 3:16

Know God's Word

Do not let this Book of the Law depart from your mouth; meditate on it day and night, so that you may be careful to do everything written in it. Then you will be prosperous and successful. Joshua 1:8

God's Adoptive Process

But to all who did receive him, who believed in his name, he gave the right to become children of God. John 1:12

Trusting God

Trust in the LORD with all your heart and lean not on your own understanding; in all your ways acknowledge him, and he will make your paths straight. Proverbs 3:5-6

Our Priority

But seek first his kingdom and his righteousness, and all these things will be given to you as well. Matthew 6:33

The Believer's Body

I appeal to you therefore, brothers, by the mercies of God, to present your bodies as a living sacrifice, holy and acceptable to God, which is your spiritual worship. Do not be conformed to this world, but be transformed by the renewal of your mind, that by testing you may discern what is the will of God, what is good and acceptable and perfect. Roman 12: 1-2

Security in Christ

For I am sure that neither death nor life, nor angels nor rulers, nor things present nor things to come, nor powers, nor height nor depth, nor anything else in all creation, will be able to separate us from the love of God in Christ Jesus our Lord. Romans 8:38-39

God's Eternal Provision

For this is the will of my Father, that everyone who looks on the Son and believes in him should have eternal life, and I will raise him up on the last day." John 6:40

The Great Commandment

Jesus replied: 'Love the Lord your God with all your heart and with all your soul and with all your mind.' This is the first and greatest commandment. And the second is like it: 'Love your neighbor as yourself.' Matthew 22:37-39

Fruit of the Spirit

But the fruit of the Spirit is love, joy, peace, patience, kindness, goodness, faithfulness, gentleness and self-control. Against such things there is no law. Galatians 5:22-23

Ellen Warren

One Way to God

Jesus answered, "I am the way and the truth and the life. No one comes to the Father except through me. John 14:6

Serving Others

Pure religion and undefiled before God and the Father is this, To visit the fatherless and widows in their affliction, and to keep himself unspotted from the world. James 1:27

Jesus Foretold

For unto us a child is born, unto us a son is given: and the government shall be upon his shoulder: and his name shall be called Wonderful, Counselor, The mighty God, The everlasting Father, The Prince of Peace. Isaiah 9:6

The Great Commission

Therefore go and make disciples of all nations, baptizing them in the name of the Father and of the Son and of the Holy Spirit, and teaching them to obey everything I have commanded you. And surely I am with you always, to the very end of the age. Matthew 28:19-20

The Nature of Love

Love is patient, love is kind. It does not envy, it does not boast, it is not proud. It is not rude, it is not self-seeking. It is not easily angered, it keeps no records of wrong. Love does not delight in evil but rejoices with the truth. It always protects, always trusts, always hopes, always perseveres. 1 Corinthians 13:4-7

True Disciples

If you hold to my teaching, you are really my disciples. Then you will know the truth, and the truth will set you free. John 8:31-32

What We Should Value

Do not store up for yourselves treasures on earth, where moth and rust destroy, and where thieves break in and steal. But store up for yourselves treasures in heaven where moth and rust do not destroy, and where thieves do not break in and steal. For where your treasure is, there your heart will be also. Matthew 6:19-21

God Keeps His Promises

Know therefore that the Lord your God is God; he is the faithful God, keeping his covenant of love to a thousand generations of those who love him and keep his commands. Deuteronomy 7:9

God Hears Us

The Lord is near to all who call on him, to all who call on him in truth. He fulfills the desires of those who fear him; he hears their cry and saves them. Psalm 145:18-19

Temptation

No temptation has seized you except what is common to man. And God is faithful; he will not let you be tempted beyond what you can bear. But when you are tempted, he will also provide a way out so that you can stand up under it. 1 Corinthians 10:13

The Beginning

In the beginning God created the heavens and the earth. Genesis 1:1

The End

Behold, I am coming soon! My reward is with me, and I will give to everyone according to what he has done. I am the Alpha and the Omega, the First and the Last, the Beginning and the End. Revelation 22:12-13

How Do I Memorize?

Here is one method of adult memorization.

1. Type up the words you wish to memorize, no matter how small. "Jesus wept." John 11:35

2. Record the words on your phone or voice recorder.

3. Listen to this segment throughout the day when accomplishing personal tasks like combing your hair, or brushing your teeth, until you feel comfortable that you can repeat the same words.

4. Practice repeating the words, then check to see if you are accurate by looking at your typed page or listening to your recording.

5. Play the recording on repeat until it is embedded into your mind.

6. Listen to the recording as you sleep that night.

7. Repeat the Scripture the next morning to confirm you have it memorized.

8. It is better to only memorize one Scripture a week, so as not to confound your memory. Repeat the Scripture every day, at least a dozen times.

Method 2 of memorization

1. Write the verse down on an index card.

2. Make multiple copies.

3. Place each copy everywhere you look up, on the front door, on the mirror, on the car visor, on your computer terminal.

4. Each time you see the verse or card, say the Scripture aloud.

5. By the end of the day this Scripture will be memorized.

Method 3 of memorization

1. Set the Scripture to music.

2. Play the song repeatedly.

3. Sing with the song.

4. You will learn the song and Scripture within 4 hours.

Chapter 11: Prayer

Prayer is the active desire to seek the face of God in fellowship and communion. If you acutely want to know the mercy and grace of God, you must seek God through prayer and meditation.

Often people make the comment that they don't know how to pray. The disciples themselves asked Jesus to teach them to pray. Here are a few ways to shape your personal prayers.

Thanksgiving

Begin your prayers thanking God for your very breath, for the presence of another day in this world, and for the promise of the Kingdom of God. Thank God for your blessings of the day, and your daily repast.

Pray for Others, Prayers of Intercession.

After you have thanked God for your day, ask for intercession in the lives of others. Name to God your concerns for unbelievers, for those who are sick and suffering. Ask God to help those who are in need, whether it be physical, emotional or spiritual. Remember that your prayers may be the prayer that touches the heart of God.

Prayer for Yourself

Lift up to God your heart's desires. Name your needs and wants. Ask for clarification of God's purpose for your life. Ask for wisdom and strength for specific tasks. Ask God to impress upon your heart how you can be an instrument for God.

Prayers for Your Country and Your Leaders

Pray for your country, for your political leaders, and for your spiritual leaders. Ask God to soften their hearts to see the oppressed, the poor, and the suffering. Ask God to strengthen your witness so that you can call the leaders accountable for their actions.

This doesn't mean that prayer is a formula and that God only hears us if we follow the correct steps. Meister Eckhart said, "If the only prayer you ever say in your entire life is thank you, it will be enough." Eckhart von Hocheim, born in Thuringia between 1250 and 1260, joined the Order of the Dominicans when he was around 18. His theological career involved founding convents, teaching, leading spiritual direction, and preaching. After some controversy in the thirteenth century when he was suspected of heresy, and some influence in the sixteenth century when Martin Luther was forging the Protestant Reformation, his writings were largely forgotten until the early nineteenth century. Eckhart preached with the goal of inspiring listeners to do good things, at a time when the church was enmeshed in political turmoil. The simplicity of his theology shows us a loving God. The God who came to Earth in the form of a baby is loving, forgiving, and approachable. Is that why, in Luke 11, one of the disciples asked for a prayer lesson?

One day, Jesus was praying in a certain place. When he finished, one of his disciples said to him, "Lord, teach us to pray, just as John taught his disciples." He said to them, 'When you pray, say:

"Father, hallowed be your name. Your kingdom come. Give us each day our daily bread, and forgive us our sins, for we ourselves forgive everyone indebted to us. And do not bring us to the time of trial."

The account in Matthew doesn't mention a disciple wanting to know how to pray. Jesus is speaking about piety and prayer as a time for privacy with God. In Matthew 6, he says, "But whenever you pray, go into your room and shut the door and pray to your Father who is in secret; and your Father who sees in secret will reward you. When you are praying, do not heap up empty phrases as the Gentiles do; for they think that they will be heard because of your many words. Do not be like them, for your Father knows what you need before you ask him. Pray then in this way: Our Father in heaven, hallowed be your name. Your kingdom come, Your will be done, on earth as it is in heaven. Give us this day our daily bread. And forgive us our debts, as we have also forgiven our debtors. And do not bring us to the time of trial, but rescue us from the evil one.

It's a very simple prayer that's prayed all over the Christian world, an authentic model for Christians to follow because it came from the Son of God, who knew what His Father Jesus himself prayed often, going off by himself to pray when he needed time away from the crowds. He prayed so intensely in the Garden of Gethsemane the night before his death that he sweated blood. Jesus had a very active prayer life; he prayed as he blessed the fishes and loaves that would feed a crowd of 5000; he prayed to

109

God before he chose the 12 men who would be his disciples; before challenging times when the Jewish authorities were hostile; before he went to the tomb where Lazarus lay wrapped in graveclothes. When his disciples asked him how to heal a madman who was possessed by an evil spirit, he explained that only prayer could drive out such a demon. Prayer was the process by which Jesus, in human form, connected with his Father in heaven for a meeting of the physical and the spiritual.

The Jewish tradition in which Jesus was raised was rich with prayer in a tradition of expression. After God parted the Red Sea and the pursuing Egyptians were drowned after the Israelites escaped, Moses sang a prayer of praise and thanks to God in Exodus 15" Who is like you, O Lord, among the gods? Who is like you, majestic in holiness, awesome in splendor, doing wonders? You stretched out your right hand, the earth swallowed them." Miriam led the women in a prayer of praise to God. Exodus records her words: "Sing to the Lord, for he has triumphed gloriously; horse and rider he has thrown into the sea."

When Deborah the judge over Israel led the forces of Barak into battle, she celebrated with prayer: "When the princes in Israel take the lead, when the people willingly offer themselves, praise the Lord!" and ending with "So may all your enemies perish, O Lord! But may they who love you be like the sun when it rises in its strength."

Prayers sometimes have a context which is very different from the words. The prayer that's known as the Mizpah Benediction reads "May the Lord watch between me and thee, while we are absent, one from the other." The holistic words of the prayer are tellingly different from the situation which inspired those words.

110

When we reflect upon the wily nature of Jacob, the son of Isaac and Rebecca, we have to admit that he came by his guile honestly as the nephew of Laban, Rebecca's brother (and as Rebecca herself proved when she helped her son deceive his blind father into giving Jacob the birthright that belonged to Esau, his older brother). Laban had tricked Jacob, who loved his cousin Rachel and wanted to wed her, into marrying the older sister, Leah. He has both sisters for wives, and then decides it's time to leave his father-in-law. Recognizing that they have cause to be suspicious of one another, their prayer, far from being a declaration of love despite distance, is the equivalent of summoning God as a witness for what they aren't in place to see. Still, for those who want to invoke the love and protection of God when they are separated, it's a beautiful prayer.

Chapter 12: Worship

Worship is the gathering of the people of God to give God praise and adoration. In a worship service, the focus is on God; included in the service are personal and intercessory prayer, the reading of Scriptures, an offering to God for the use of His Kingdom and servants, a responsive reading of the Psalms through song or repetition, songs of praise, an expository sermon or talk regarding God or the Scripture, corporate prayers, and prayers of confession. Many pastors follow the lectionary readings which assign designated scriptures throughout the worship year. The purpose of this is so that the reading of the scriptures is not restricted to certain verses but includes the Bible as a complete resource. The lectionary cycle is in three years, and during that span of time, verses of the Old and New Testament will be read to the congregation.

Worship is necessary to strengthen the Christian spirit through enhancement of spiritual things. Jesus, in the book of Matthew, encourages believers and followers to "come together" 27 times. Jesus knew that people are strengthened by fellowship and worship.

What should you look for in a church home or fellowship?

Look for a form of worship in which you are comfortable physically. If you do not like to wear formal clothing, pick a church that is a "come as you are church." If instead you prefer to "dress your best" on Sunday, pick a church that encourages giving your best at worship. If you are disabled and mobility challenged, pick a church that is on one level and easily accessible so that you can come and go to the different areas of the worship center. Keep in mind that many churches offer both a traditional worship service and a contemporary or less formal service. By visiting a church with multiple services, you will be able to determine which style best suits your worship needs.

Listen to the style of worship to discern that it both challenges and compels you to increase your Christian faith. Does the music uplift you? Or does the music bore you and leave your mind wandering? Find a church that has music that increases your energy and commitment to God, not one that bores you or leaves you disinterested. Are you someone who cherishes the familiar hymns, or someone who prefers praise songs? Many services offer a mix of both, but you will want to experience the worship service to decide for yourself whether the music meets your spiritual needs.

Does the church leader preach the Word of God? Are the sermons taken from Scripture or are they psychobabble or social commentary? Be careful to discern that you are being fed the Word of God, and instead of a salesman giving you life lessons in prosperity. Look for a church leader that is an example of a godly man or woman, one that models self as Jesus. If the preacher is flashy, prone to designer clothing or jewelry, or known to live in a mansion and drive expensive cars, question if that pastor is following God closely. Ask to whom the pastor and the treasury is accountable. If the church does not have open business or board meetings, ask why not. Finding out the form of government which the church follows is very important. Is there a governing board which represents the congregation and is responsive to the voice of the people? Does the pastor make decisions on his or her own or is there an elected council?

Does the pastor use the pulpit as a means of promoting political views? Remember that Bible-based preaching may include the headlines, but does not tell congregation members how to vote or for whom to vote. Theologian Karl Barth said, in a 1963 article published in *Time* magazine: "Take your Bible and take your newspaper, and read both. But interpret newspapers from your Bible." In an era of polarizing politics, religion has been used to bolster candidates in a way that does no credit to the Christian creed. As a Christian, it's sometimes difficult to know how to discern a political candidate's beliefs from his actions. As a voter, you cast your ballot for the candidate who represents your political causes. Are your political beliefs consistent with what the Bible says, keeping in mind that the Bible includes many verses which espouse a variety of different scenarios. Lot's daughters had sexual relations with their father: does that mean that the Bible endorses incest? Of course not. Jephthah sacrificed his daughter: does that prove that God approves of child sacrifice? Of course not. Know your Bible and you will not be deceived by the wolves in sheep's clothing who seek to deceive the flock of Jesus. And if you are in doubt, rely upon the words in Micah 6:8: "What does the Lord require of you but to do justice, and to love kindness, and to walk humbly with your God?"

Watch the members of the church to see if they form cliques or tight-knit groups that have no room for outsiders. Look to see if there are opportunities for service in the close community and in the greater world. If the church is not meeting the needs of the outside community, it is just a social club with exclusive membership. Are people of other ethnic groups welcome in the church? Martin Luther King, Jr. once said that Sunday morning is the most segregated hour of the week in the United States. Does the church welcome people of different races, origins, backgrounds, socioeconomic status, and education? B Belonging to a church should never be seen as a status symbol.

Choose carefully and then become involved. Offer yourself for service. Remember the words of Paul in First Corinthians 12: Now there are varieties of gifts, but the same Spirit; and there are varieties of service, but the same Lord; and there are varieties of activities, but it is the same God who activates all of them in everyone. To each is given the manifestation of the Spirit for the common good. To one is given . . . the utterance of wisdom, and to another the utterance of knowledge . . ., to another faith . . . to another gifts of healing . . . to another the working of miracles . . ... to another prophecy, to another the discernment of spirits . . . to another various kinds of tongues, to another the interpretation of tongues." Pauls' list may seem to be quite different from what churches today need, but whether your talents come from your ability to teach pre-schoolers about Jesus in simple terms that they can understand, or whether your gifts come in the form of a hammer and nails that are used to build a ramp for the handicapped, the church needs you.

God rejoices in human diversity! Everybody can do something. It may be you that God has picked you to mind the nursery, light the candles, sing in the choir, or open a food pantry. Maybe God is calling you to do repair work gratis for the church elderly, drive a person to the grocery store, or pick up prescriptions for the sick. Not every person who serves has a visible role in the church. The important part is that you increase your service, as a repayment of gratitude for what God has done for you. Remember that the gifts you have came from God; what better way to show your appreciation than to share those gifts with others in need.

Worship is both spiritually nourishing and physically restorative. A New York Times op-ed article published on April 20, 2013 lists the health benefits of church attendance, which has been credited as boosting the immune system and decreasing blood pressure, adding two-three years to life expectancy. Evangelical groups that support one another through a personal network of compassion. Regular church attendance seems to promote healthier behaviors that include less smoking and drinking of alcohol, drug use, and less sexual promiscuity. The author of the article, T.M. Luhrmann, observed that faith requires its believers to experience the world as something more than material and observable. Luhrmann cites studies which show that, when a person perceives his or her relationship with God to be positive, close and intimate, the person suffered less illness and decreased stress.

That does not mean that people who attend church are immune to suffering and sickness. What it means is that people who are ill, alone, frightened, and lost have someone to turn to in the form of a God who cares about their personal wellbeing. "I am with you always," Jesus promised. Believers, through their personal relationship with God and the support system of other church members, find community in their faith.

Chapter 13: Finding Comfort in the Bible

The book of Psalms is the one to which believers are directed during times of personal trial. Outside of the gospels, where we see God-with-us, Emmanuel, as a man in the presence of ordinary men and women, the Psalms are perhaps the best Biblical source for that blend of divine and mortal. The Psalms show human beings in all manifestations of their relationship to God and one another: the praise is fervent; the despair desolate; the anger boiling; the joy exuberant. The Psalms are both sermons in miniature and a form of literature, so it's natural that they appeal on different levels.

Although they are part of the Old Testament, the Psalms are frequently referred to in the New Testament because they are part of the spine of Scriptures. Fourth century church leader Athanasius is credited with stating that the Psalms "have a unique place in the Bible because most of the Scripture speaks to us while the Psalms speak for us." The Psalms are the script by which the people of both the Old and the New Testament speak to God.

The 150 psalms are divided into five sections:

Psalms	1-41
Psalms	42-72
Psalms	73-89
Psalms	90-106
Psalms 107-150	

The psalms are designed to cover a gamut of emotions: repentance of sins and confidence in God's forgiveness; psalms of praise which rejoice in God's providence and goodness; psalms of ascent for worshippers going to the Temple in Jerusalem; lamentations which express despair, anger and pleas for help from God; psalms of wisdom which compare good and evil and those who follow the paths which lead to God's pleasure or God's punishment; songs of the king, which delineate the role of the king in his role as spiritual leader.

This categorization of the Book of Psalms shows up in all the original manuscripts, although scholars aren't sure why. It's possible that there is some chronology involved, with the first segment consisting of the oldest psalms.

Old and New Testaments express their faith in God, even when that faith is tested, as it was when Jesus was in agony on the cross and he recited a verse from Psalm 22:1, "My God, my God, why have you abandoned me?" In fact, the New Testament quotes from the Psalms over 75 times; the Book of Romans alone, the work of the Apostle Paul, quotes from Psalms 14 times.

The psalms for which David is credited with writing are laments, many of them from the period in his life when he was escaping the wrath of King Saul. We think of David as the psalm writer and the king, forgetting that before he ascended to the throne, he had to fight for the kingship.

Martin Luther, the leader of the Protestant Reformation, believed that the Psalms taught Christians more about prayer. The Christian can learn to pray in the psalter, for her he can hear how the saints talk with God. The number of moods which are expressed here, joy and suffering, hope and care, make it possible for every Christian to find himself in it, and to pray with the psalms."

During the nightmare of the Nazi years, the Lutheran minister Dietrich Bonhoeffer, who was involved in a plot to assassinate Adolf Hitler and was imprisoned, brought a copy of Luther's translations of the Psalms with him to prison. As he awaited execution, he wrote on the Psalms and found comfort in them. He wrote, "I am reading the Psalms daily, as I have done for years." According to a friend, even as the end of his life approached, Bonhoeffer continued to exude a feeling of joy despite the circumstances in which he found himself. His friend observed that he was "one of the very few men that I have ever met to whom his God was real and close to him."

The Twenty-Third Psalm

Perhaps the most famous of the psalms, this psalm, written by David, is the psalm of comfort. It's read at funerals to console grieving families, but its verses bring hope to the living, the suffering, and the struggling, as well. It begins with the timeless words that inspire solace and a promise of safety: the Lord is my shepherd, I shall not want. Its images are vivid, and the comparison of God to a shepherd evokes both David's past and the role of Jesus as the Good Shepherd. To be a shepherd is not an exalted role but even as a king, David understood the nurturing role of the shepherd who protected his flock, as he had done in his youth, who went in search of the sheep that was lost, as Jesus does. The imagery is brilliant: God takes care of his believers and even in the presence of enemies, prepares a table. God is the provider and protector.

Psalm 1

The first psalm is an introduction into the way of right-living: "Happy are those who do not follow the advice of the wicked," the psalmist writes, "or take the path that sinners tread." Their reward will be long-lasting: "They are like trees planted by streams of water, which yield their fruit in its season, and their leaves do not wither. In all that they do, they prosper." A tree is buffeted by storms; its branches fall, it sheds its leaves as sunny autumn days give way to barren winter. But the tree prospers. So it is, the psalmist says, with those who do what is right in God's eyes. It's not so for the wicked; they, like chaff, will be driven away. The way is clear, Psalm 1 advises: follow in the steps of the godly and reap the blessings of the God who rewards the faithful. Follow in the steps of the ungodly, and sow the harvest of misfortune.

Psalm 40

Waiting is hard and waiting for God can be even harder. No matter how many times we concede that God's time is not our time, we are impatient for a response. In Psalm 40, David writes that he waited patiently for the Lord at a time when he was in a desolate pit. Given the circumstances of David's life, the pit could be either metaphorical or actual; there's no denying that the son of Jesse managed to get himself into difficult situations in both his personal and royal life. But this psalm, while it acknowledges that life is full of evil and difficulties, and that our sin leads us into peril, proudly asserts the magnificence of God, His power and His mercy. What does God want from his faithful servants? Obedience. Recognizing this, David speaks triumphantly of God's ability and willingness to deliver a sinful man from peril. And then, because David is human and not diving, the psalm ends with a reminder of human impatience: "You are my help and my deliverer; do not delay, o my God.

Psalm 46

Also known as Luther's psalm because the leader of the Protestant Reformation was one he sang during difficult times in his life, Psalm 46 addresses not a personal crisis but a corporate one, a time of national calamity. This is not one of the Psalms for which David is credited with authorship; no one knows who the sons of Korah are, but scholars believed that the psalms accredited to them were written after David's reign. Psalm 46 reminds the fearful or faint-hearted that God will not abandon the faithful. "Therefore we will not fear, though the earth should change, though the mountains shake in the heart of the sea; though its water roar and foam, though the mountains tremble with its tumult." Despite the tumult which the city finds itself, God is within the city, and his comfort is unassailable. "Be still, and know that I am God!"

Chapter 14: Forgiveness

Then Peter came to Jesus and asked, "Lord, how many times shall I forgive my brother or sister who sins against me? Up to seven times?"

Jesus answered, "I tell you, not seven times, but seventy times seven."

When Peter asked Jesus whether forgiving seven times was sufficient, he was being generous. But the answer that he received was not what he or any righteous person would have expected.

To forgive seventy times seven-which doing the math reveals to be a whopping 490 times—must have seemed excessive to even the most tolerant of believers. But Jesus, with his unique insights into the human conditions, understood what Peter did not, which was that God's forgiveness has no limit. During his ministry, Jesus practiced what he preached. It also got him into trouble with the Jewish authorities.

People had come to see the miracle worker of whom so much had been heard. The city was crowded; some to hear a holy man, some to enjoy the spectacle. There were men who had brought a friend to Jesus for healing; the friend was paralyzed. They could not get through to Jesus because the crowd of people was a barricade, but this didn't stop them. They went to the roof of the house where he was based and lowered him through the roof, down into the crowd in front of Jesus. Jesus was impressed d by the friends and their faith. He said to the man, "Your sins are forgiven."

A strange thing, one would assume, to say to a paralyzed man. The Pharisees were offended; they tended to be easily offended by anything which broke from their rigid standards of religious decorum. Who was this person, they wondered, who took on the role of God and forgave sins? Jesus knew what they were thinking—indeed, we can only imagine the body language, the scowls, the various ways in which they indicated their disapproval.

Jesus confronted them. "Which is easier: to say your sins are forgiven," he asks in Luke 5, "or to say 'Get up and walk'? The Son of Man, he told them, has the authority to forgive sins. He then told the man to pick up his mat and go home." The crowd was amazed. The Pharisees, of course, were not pleased. Oblivious to the healing that had taken place, they counted Jesus as a blasphemer.

Jesus was a threat to the Old Guard which held a tight-fisted grip on religious authority. But he was also a threat to the social fabric which ruled the Jewish community and at no point was this more apparent than when he was summoned by the Pharisees who had what they regarded as incontrovertible proof of sin which surely, this Galilean troublemaker would have to concur with their judgment. An adulteress, caught in the act. The sentence was clear: Mosaic Law said that she was to die by stoning.

Mysteriously, Jesus bent down and, using his finger, wrote something in the sand while the Pharisees waited for him to side with them. But he rose, and said, "Let the one who has never sinned cast the first stone." Bending down, he continued to write in the sand.

The self-righteous judges gradually drifted away. Who could claim to be without sin? When the only people left were Jesus and the adulteress, he stood up. "Where are your accusers? Didn't even one of them condemn you?"

They had not.

"Neither do I condemn you. Go and sin no more."

Women were easy targets in the ancient world. The patriarchal society kept women in a subservient role with the full approbation of the religious hierarchy. Jesus included women among his followers, and he afforded them a respect that was alien to the times. But to address a clearly defined sin, one which was listed among the ten "thou shalt nots" and to do it in such a way that the trained scholars could not refute him, showed a boldness for which the Pharisees were not prepared. Jesus, the sinless one, did not condemn the woman who sinned. He told her to sin no more. And she lived because of him.

Perhaps his most famous pronouncement of forgiveness came when he was seemingly at his least powerful. There they stood, a trio of criminals on crosses, condemned by the Romans to die for their crimes. Two thieves, one on each side of the man sent reluctantly by Pilate to die, shared the shame, pain and desolation of that shameful death. One thief mocked Jesus: if you're the son of God, what are you doing here? Save yourself if you can. But the other thief rebuked him. "This man is innocent. We are not. We are here to die for what we did. He is dying for doing nothing wrong." Believing in the power of the Lord, he asked Jesus to remember him in heaven. And Jesus promised that the thief would join him in paradise."

The instinct to forgive is so strong in God that even when his Son was dying on the cross, he extended his blessing to a sinner. If there's doubt that God loves us beyond our deserving, those words on the cross convince us. And if they do not, consider how Jesus reacted to the soldiers who nailed him to the cross, mocked him with their jibes, rolled dice for his garments and quenched his thirst with sour wine. "Father, forgive them; they don't know what they're doing."

The blessings of our God, who knows what He is doing when we misplace our faith and follow our own flawed inclinations, is always stronger than our will. The Bible shows us that forgiveness is a habit we are accepted to adopt and never break.

Seventy times seven. Eternal forgiveness. God's example.

Chapter 15: Did You Know?

Hollywood and the entertainment media have mined the early books of the Bible for a lively and lucrative rendition of biblical stories. The story of Jacob's daughter Dinah was barely biblical common knowledge until the publication of the novel *The Red Tent* by Anita Diamant. Published in 1997, and filmed as a miniseries in 2014, *The Red Tent* recounts the lives of the women who lived behind the scenes, often not even named.

Moses has been portrayed in film by Charlton Heston in the 1956 film *The Ten Commandments* and by Christian Bale in the 2014 film *Exodus: Gods and Kings*. Russell Crowe brought the flood story of *Noah* to the silver screen in 2014. Music maestro Andrew Lloyd Webber turned the tale of Joseph into *Joseph and the Amazing Technicolor Dreamcoat* in 1968.

From the earliest days of the motion picture industry through modern times, the Bible has served as a mother lode of inspiration for films. And not only for films. When John Steinbeck needed a title for his classic novel about the good-and-evil Trask brothers, he chose *East of Eden*; the location where Cain was exiled after the murder of his brother.

Far from serving up a sanitized version of a holy people, the early books do not deny the actions of the people whose lives are recorded. After their mother is turned into a pillar of salt for looking back as the city of Sodom is destroyed, the daughters fear that they will never bear children. They get their father Lot, drunk, and have intercourse with him in order to become pregnant.

After the Flood, when Noah and his family have returned to dry land, Noah is not averse to enjoying the fruit of the vine. Sampling the wine of his vineyard, he becomes drunk and, somewhere in the process, naked. For looking upon his father's nakedness, taboo in those times, his son Ham is cursed. The passage later was conveniently, if unofficially, interpreted as the Bible's endorsement of slavery. If Ham was cursed and his skin turned black for his violation of his father's privacy, practitioners of slavery took this as vindication of their ownership of dark-skinned Africans.

The allure of Bathsheba at her bath which so captivated King David that he sent for her was equally enticing for artists; the scene was a popular Renaissance painting theme and was also depicted by Rembrandt.

The William Faulkner novel *Absalom, O Absalom*, is taken from the lament of David at the death of his son: "Oh my son Absalom, my son, my son Absalom! Would God I had died for thee, O Absalom, my son, my son!"

Widely regarded as the most evil of all the queens who married into the Israelite royal family, Jezebel, wife of King Ahab, came to a particularly gruesome fate for her sins. She was thrown from a window; when the king who ordered her death sent his servants to bury her, all that was left was her skull, feet, the palms of her hands, and her blood. The dogs, as predicted by the prophet Elijah, had devoured her.

It's unfortunate that Solomon didn't write the Book of Proverbs.

Proverbs 31:10-31 outlines the qualities which make the perfect wife. The views of a man who had 700 wives on what made a perfect one would certainly have been interesting.

Ecclesiastes made it to the top of the charts! Pete Seeger wrote music for *Turn, Turn, Turn (To Everything There is a Season)* in the 1950s. In 1965, the song was recorded by the American musical group The Byrds, making it a number one hit with lyrics thousands of years old.

Isaiah is the longest of the books written by the major prophets, with 66 chapters, while the shortest book by minor prophet Obadiah consists of a single chapter.

Jeremiah's writing style added a word to the dictionary: a jeremiad is described as a lament, a complaint, or a prophecy of doom.

The Book of Daniel contains several phrases which continue to have meaning in modern times. The "handwriting on the wall" refers to Chapter 5's words written by a disembodied hand upon the walls of the Babylonian king's palace. Daniel is called to interpret the writing; he explains that the words mean that the Babylonian kingdom will come to an end at the conquering hands of the Persians.

Daniel also interprets another biblical phrase "You have been weighed in the balance and found wanting." It's an indictment of Belshazzar, the grandson of Nebuchadnezzar, who allowed his dinner guests to drink from cups taken from the Jewish temple.

Malachi's name appears nowhere else in the Bible, leading scholars to believe that it's not a reference to a name and therefore the author may be anonymous.

John, the beloved disciple, is a character in Dan Brown's best-selling novel *The Da Vinci Code*; in the novel, John is actually a woman, and the beloved of Jesus. Although an examination of the da Vinci painting *The Last Supper* does show John with effeminate features, this was a practice of the Renaissance artists to indicate someone of youth. The popularity of the novel and movie led to renewed speculation about Jesus and whether he was married or celibate.

The crucifixion story has provided Western literature with memorable phrases:

- "30 pieces of silver" refers to the money Judas was paid for his betrayal.
- "Washing his hands of the matter" refers to Pilate, who when pronouncing sentence upon Jesus, washed his hands in a basin to indicate his innocence.
- "The rooster crowed" refers to Peter's denial of Christ, three times before the rooster crowed.
- "Thy will be done" is spoken by Jesus when, after an agonizing night of prayer and fear, knowing that crucifixion is upon him, he begs God to free him from his fate. At the end, he surrenders to God's will.
- "Today you will be with me in paradise": Jesus' words to the thief beside him on the cross, who proclaims that Jesus is innocent of wrongdoing.

130

Christianity is named for Jesus Christ, whose teachings its followers practice, but if not for Paul and his letters, the religion would have been deprived of its most outspoken advocate. The movement of the religion from a Jewish sect to a religion in its own right, which although still claiming a Jewish foundation adopted a different set of beliefs, would not have taken place. The emphasis which Paul placed on converting the Gentiles would not have happened. Almost half of the 27 books in the New Testament are credited to Paul, although scholars doubt that he was the author of all of them. It's believed that Romans, First and Second Corinthians, Galatians, Philippians, First Thessalonians, and Philemon were dictated by him. Although he may not have written him, the letters are not false; they may have been written by his followers, or by people who had access to his writings.

Although Paul is often quoted for his comments which indicate that women should be subservient to men in the church leadership, it's also true that his mention of women in his letters shows a respect for their participation in the church. The Christian faith attracted a number of women to its ranks and Paul welcomed them to the ministry of Christ.

Although popes are required to be unmarried, we know that at one point in his life, Peter had a mother-in-law. We know this because Jesus cured her illness during his ministry. It was a time when women and wives were mentioned if their existence had bearing on the events. Whether Peter was still a husband later in his ministry, we don't know. Tradition says that when he was crucified, Peter felt that he did not deserve the honor of being crucified in the same manner as Jesus, and he requested to be upside down.

Revelation has inspired not only theologians but also writers as diverse as Christina Rossetti and D.H. Lawrence

The notion of the Rapture, the belief that those who believe in Christ will suddenly leave earth in the midst of their daily life, comes from Paul in his first letter to the Thessalonians. Paul's focus was on the resurrection and return to Christ, not on the mayhem that would result from the random disappearance of the saved.

The Book of Psalms contains both the shortest (Psalm 117) and the longest chapters (Psalm 119) of Scripture and also includes the exact center of the Bible. If you open your Bible to the center, it will open to chapter 118, the center of the Bible. Psalms 118:8 is the center verse of the Bible: It is better to trust in the Lord than to put confidence in man." Before Psalm 118, there are 594 chapters; following Psalm 118, there are 594 chapters.

Chapter 17: Conclusions

Within this book, we have discussed many topics important to the Christian faith. Although the book was written to make understanding the Bible easier, it was also written to enhance your spiritual life so that you will desire to seek the Kingdom of God.

If you have not made a personal commitment to God, we ask that you take this time to share with God a renewal of your faith. Tell God about your sinful nature, confess your wrongdoings, your sins of omission and commission, and then ask for the saving grace of Jesus Christ to redeem you from your sins. Commit to finding a worship center that will educate and enlighten your spirit.

It is time now to commit to a Bible reading plan, a vibrant worship center, and a rich personal prayer life. Finding a place where you and challenged to grow and serve is a stimulating part of the Christian walk. Banding with other Christians will strengthen your personal commitment and your faithful witness. Are you ready for this exciting journey in faith?

Knowing about the Bible is another way of knowing more about your world. The Bible, from its ancient origins to its modern interpretation, is the autobiography of the Christian family. Your study of the Bible, from the miscellaneous facts to the deepest revelations, will not only teach you more about God: it will teach you more about yourself.

Appendix 1: Where to find help in the Scriptures

Afraid	Psalm 34:4 Matthew 10:28 II Timothy 1:7 Hebrews 13:5,6	Needing God's Protection	Psalm 27:1-6 Psalm 91 Philippians 4:19
Anxious	Psalm 46 Matthew 6:19-34 Philippians 4:6 I Peter 5:6,7	Needing Guidance	Psalm 32:8 Proverbs 3:5,6
Backsliding	Psalm 51 I John 1:4-9	Needing Peace	John 14:1-4 John 16:33 Romans 5:1-5 Philippians 4:6,7
Bereaved	Matthew 5:4 II Corinthians 1:3,4	Needing Rules for Living	Romans 12
Bitter or Critical	I Corinthians 13	Overcome	Psalm 6 Romans 8:31-39 Romans 5:1-5 I John 1:4-9
Conscious of Sin	Proverbs 28:13	Prayerful	Psalm 4 Psalm 42 Luke 11:1-13 John 17

			I John 5:14,15
Defeated	Romans 8:31-39	Protected	Psalm 18:1-3 Psalm 34:7
Depressed	Psalm 34	Sick or in Pain	Psalm 38 Matthew 26:39 Romans 5:3-5 II Corinthians 12:9,10 I Peter 4:12,13,19
Disaster Threatens	Psalm 91 Psalm 118:5,6 Luke 8:22:-25	Sorrowful	Psalm 51 Matthew 5:4 John 14 II Corinthians 1:3,4 I Thessalonians 4:13-18
Discouraged	Psalm 23 Psalm 42:6-11 Psalm 55:22 Matthew 5:11,12 II Corinthians 4:8-18 Philippians 4:4-7	Tempted	Psalm 1 Psalm 139:23,24 Matthew 26:41 I Corinthians 10:12-14 Philippians 4:8 James 4:7 II Peter 2:9 II Peter 3:17
Doubting	Matthew 8:26 Hebrews 11	Thankful	Psalm 100 I Thessalonians 5:18

			Hebrews 13:15
Facing a Crisis	Psalm 121 Matthew 6:25-34 Hebrews 4:16	Traveling	Psalm 121
Faith Fails	Psalm 42:5 Hebrews 11	In Trouble	Psalm 16 Psalm 31 John 14:1-4 Hebrews 7:25
Friends Fail	Psalm 41:9-13 Luke 17:3,4 Romans 12:14,17,19,21 II Timothy 4:16-18	Weary	Psalm 90 Matthew 11:28-30 I Corinthians 15:58 Galatians 6:9,10
Leaving Home	Psalm 121 Matthew 10:16-20	Worried	Matthew 6:19-34 I Peter 5:6,7
Lonely	Psalm 23 Hebrews 13:5,6		

http://stmarksunnyvale.org/bible/bible_reference/bible_topic/bv _where_to_find_help.html

**** PREVIEW OTHER BOOKS BY THIS AUTHOR****

[Excerpt from the first 2 Chapters]

"MEN THAT CHANGED THE COURSE OF HISTORY" by Dominique Atkinson

Introduction

The 21st century stands witness to the achievements of some of the most influential men in the world. And yet, no matter how today's movers and shakers stand in contemporary rankings, how can we compare them to the giants of the past, the men who took history in their bare hands and bent it to their will? Whether they strode upon the stages of military power or at the altars of religious belief, they have left their marks on civilization.

Accustomed as we are to the rule of law, we risk forgetting that the legend of Moses the Lawgiver and his acquisition of the Ten Commandments is the landmark event in Jewish pre-history. Those original stone tablets have been the midwife to numerous judicial children, blending the obligations of moral law with the requirements of civil and criminal law in a succinct body.

Bill Gates and Microsoft transformed the way in which data could be collected and compiled; when Gates retired to leave his desktop empire behind in favor of philanthropy, was it because he was ready for a new phase in his life or was it because, as the legend says of Alexander the Great, there were no worlds left to

137

conquer?

How would Constantine's predecessor, Julius Caesar, have reacted if he'd known that over 300 years after his reign, a subsequent emperor would turn his back on the Roman gods and embrace Christianity, a religion that began with the ministry of an obscure carpenter from an insignificant region of the empire and evolved into a faith practiced by billions? And, centuries later, how does the upstart Corsican Napoleon rank as the military leader who created an empire with himself as its head, reminiscent of Caesar, and redesigned his nation?

How do the advances made by cell phone technology that have been so integral to the Apple empire founded by the late Steve Jobs compare to the letters, journeys, and missionary zeal of Saint Paul, who traveled with that obscure carpenter's story across thousands of miles, braving shipwrecks, pirates, prison, and ultimately, execution?

What was the force in the desert that stirred up the Prophet Mohammed and inspired the birth of a religion whose believers will make up more than an estimated 50 percent of the population in 50 countries?

The names of these men have echoed through the halls of history since their exploits reconfigured the maps, laws, beliefs, and annals of the past. Today we live in a world shaped by their footprints. But what do we know of these game-changers? Immersed as we are in social media, headlines, 24-hour news and the Internet, how can we effectively evaluate the parts that these men played when they occupied the stage of world events?

Chapter One: Moses the Lawgiver

Who was Moses?

Moses never went to law school. Nor did he have any prior experience as a tour guide. It's obvious that the man who led his travelers on a 40-year journey through the wilderness lacked a GPS; cynics might even say that he lacked any sense of direction. But Moses was not appointed by God to lead the people of Israel because of his navigational skills. He was charged not only with freeing an enslaved people but with forging them into a nation: 12 tribes with a primitive awareness of one deity, transformed into a people whose commitment to the law and to monotheism would give them the skills they would need to survive in a world that all too often proved hostile.

Moses stands tall in an ancient time when men and myth frequently merged, until the saga becomes embedded in truth, regardless of what can be proven. Archeologists, historians, and theologians cannot reach a consensus about the man who is revered by the three major monotheistic religions of Judaism, Christianity, and Islam. His life is estimated to have taken place as long ago as 1500 years before the birth of Jesus Christ, but a man of this stature bestows upon the millennia a sense of eternity because his legacy, the Ten Commandments, is as relevant now as when the tablets first appeared.

It's not as though there were no laws before Moses. After all, Hammurabi's Code established a legal system for the Babylonians approximately several centuries before Moses is estimated to have made his appearance. However, Hammurabi's legal doctrine was more of a civil structure than Moses' laws, which were based upon the moral code ordained by God. Viewed in another light, there are no Hollywood movies starring A-list actors telling the story of Hammurabi. *Exodus*, the story of Moses starring Christian Bale, was a Hollywood blockbuster. And before Bale, there was Charlton Heston taking on the role of the Hebrew leader in The Ten *Commandments*. But who is the character of Moses outside of today's silver screen and the Bible?

In the Beginning

Moses entered history in the Old Testament Book of Exodus at a time when his people, the Israelites, who went to Egypt generations before to escape a famine, had been downgraded from royal favorites to royal slaves. The Egyptian pharaoh, fearing that the fertility of the Israelites would overwhelm the population of his country, decided upon a ruthless solution. The midwives were ordered by the pharaoh to let infant girls live, but to kill the boys. The Bible says that the midwives obeyed God, and refused to kill the baby boys. Their response, when asked by the pharaoh why the Israelites continued to have male children, was that Hebrew women gave birth before the midwives arrived.

A modern saying asserts that behind every great man is a great woman. Moses' early life was a testimonial to these words because his very existence depended upon the courage of women: first the brave midwives who risked pharaoh's ire to protect the children they delivered, and then his mother Jochebed, who defied the decree. When her baby boy was born, the Book of Exodus tells us that she placed her son in a basket in the reeds on the banks of the Nile. When the pharaoh's daughter went to bathe in the river, she found the basket and adopted the baby, naming him Moses, an Egyptian and not a Hebrew name. Exodus relates that Moses' older sister Miriam, conveniently on

140

site when the baby was discovered, offered to find an Israelite nurse for the baby. The royal infant's biological mother was the nurse; it's easy to see that Moses came from a most resourceful family, with female relatives who knew how to maneuver in a dangerous world. That resourcefulness would stand Moses in good stead in the years to come.

Early Influences

As a member of the royal household, Moses lived a life of privilege. We know nothing of those early years, although cinematic accounts have created scenes which, while entertaining, fail to fill in the gaps. However, he was aware of his own heritage, and knew that he was not an Egyptian by birth. What we do know is that, one day, when Moses saw an Egyptian beating an Israelite, he lost his temper—Moses' temper would get the better of him more than once—and killed the Egyptian. His act was not appreciated by his people; when Moses tried to break up a fight between two Israelite slaves, one of the men challenged him by asking him if he intended to kill him as he had the Egyptian.

Moses had not concealed his act as well as he thought. Some scholars believe that when Moses was an adult, the ruling pharaoh was Thutmose III, a brilliant military tactician with a history of ruthless actions. Moses apparently felt—correctly, as it turned out—that his quasi-royal status would not save him from the wrath of the pharaoh. With his life in danger from the pharaoh, Moses fled from Egypt and made his way to Midian in northwestern Arabia.

Moses began a new life in a new land. He had made a good impression by coming to the rescue of seven young women when

141

shepherds tried to prevent them from watering their flocks of sheep. Moses married Zipporah, one of the seven, and began a family. His life must have seemed a far cry from his daily routine in Midian, but his destiny seemed to be decided; he was a husband, a father, a shepherd. But the situation in Egypt had not changed, even though he was no longer a part of it; although he was distant from the scene, the cruelty to the Israelites had only increased.

Moses' Life Changes

One day, while tending to his father-in-law's flocks, Moses had a visit from a being whose status surpassed anything at the Egyptian court. He saw a bush on fire, but he could tell that nothing was burning. Intrigued, Moses went closer. But not too close—a voice from the bush told him not to come nearer because he was on holy ground. And then came an introduction that was to change the course of history. "I am the God of your father, the God of Abraham, the God of Isaac, and the God of Jacob." Frightened, Moses hid his face.

God then proceeded to conduct one of the most unusual job interviews ever recorded. Moses, God said, was to go to Egypt and rescue the Israelite slaves so that he could bring them to freedom in a prosperous new land. Moses wanted to know, logically enough, why he was the one to do this task. God answered the question behind the question, telling Moses that God would be with him. But Moses was by no means easy to convince. He reminded God that God had been a stranger to the Israelites; they would need to be introduced. God provided the introductory information. But Moses proved his mettle by continuing to probe God. What if they didn't believe that Moses was sent by God? He reminded God that he wasn't eloquent (Moses was said to stutter). Moses asked how he could convince the Israelites that he was sent by God to deliver them from the Egyptians.

Suddenly it was God who had to present his credentials. He transformed Moses' staff into a serpent and then back into a staff; he afflicted Moses' hand with leprosy and then healed it. But Moses didn't capitulate, another trait that would serve him well when he was facing an intransigent monarch in Egypt. Moses explained again that he wasn't a smooth talker; he would need help if he were to take on this mission. Finally, God agreed to allow Moses' older brother Aaron to accompany Moses on this mission.

Aaron was Moses' intermediary with the Israelites, convincing them that God intended to rescue them from bondage. But the pharaoh was not so obliging. Stubbornly he refused to release his slaves, even though his land was cursed by a series of plagues. Until the last, terrible, inevitable plague. The tenth plague sent the Angel of Death to the households of the Egyptians but passed over the Israelite homes, an event commemorated in the symbolic holiday of Passover. Grieving at the death of his heir and the monumental loss of life, the pharaoh released the Israelites from captivity and they began their journey from enslavement to freedom under Moses' leadership. But then the pharaoh changed his mind, called for his warriors and chariots, galloped off in pursuit of his escaping slaves, and nearly overtook them. Then Moses raised his staff, and the waters of the Red Sea parted, allowing the Israelites to cross on dry land. But when the Egyptians followed, the walls of water engulfed them and they drowned.

Life, however, would prove to be very different on the other side of the sea, as Moses became a full-time nanny to a people who had grown so accustomed to enslavement that, instead of rejoicing in their liberation, they berated their liberator because their meals no longer had the same seasonings and flavor as those they enjoyed in Egypt. For the sake of a good meal, it seemed, the Israelites were ready to relinquish their freedom.

Their complaints and accusations sorely tried Moses' patience. It became Moses' task to teach the former slaves that with freedom came responsibility, both to one another and to God. He went up to Mount Sinai to receive the stone tablets upon which were written the laws that God had decreed his people were to live by.

Moses' leadership encompassed a variety of roles as the Israelites made their way from slavery to freedom. But God had told Moses that he would not be the one to take the people to their new homeland. The prophet who taught his people to be a nation died on Mount Nebo, where legend says that his grave was dug by God. For the Jews, no other prophet compares to him.

Why Moses Matters
Moses received the Ten Commandments from God; the first four commandments are based on religion; the fifth commandment concerns family responsibility; the sixth and eighth address the crimes of murder and theft; the seventh, ninth, and tenth focus on moral living: don't commit adultery, don't lie, and don't covet the belongings of others. It's a succinct body of law, but from it comes the foundation of our concept of justice and morality. The books of Deuteronomy and Leviticus provided more detailed laws

for living as a people, but it's the Ten Commandments that altered history. They came down from Mount Sinai, they were held intact along with Christian precepts that would come much later. They traveled across oceans and seas, and took root in countries and continents far distant from the land of milk and honey where the Israelites would claim a home.

The legacy of Moses is lasting. The American Supreme Court pays tribute to Moses the Lawgiver. Above the back entrance where the Supreme Court meets, Moses is one of three figures in the frieze, taking his place in history for his bequest to humanity; he's holding blank tablets which bring to mind the Ten Commandments. Throughout the world, as laws are made and challenged, the contribution of Moses to the vitality of both legal courts and personal conscience remains a bulwark of jurisprudence.

Chapter Two: Alexander the Great

Who was Alexander?

Alexander, the Great never went to military school. But he had a pedigree that would be the envy of any West Point cadet, and a claim to fame that four-star generals would covet. This martial wunderkind was never defeated in battle. His native Macedon's boundaries were unable to contain him; Alexander conquered much of what was regarded as the known world at the time: Egypt, Mesopotamia, Anatolia, Syria, Phoenicia, Judea, and Gaza, reaching as far as India and covering 3000 miles of land. The only reason that his conquests ended at India was because his troops had had enough of wandering and battle, and they wanted to return home.

In the Beginning
Home was Macedon. His father Philip II was the king of Macedon; it was his principal wife, one of a handful of women also married to Philip, who gave birth to Alexander, on a memorable day when her husband had been victorious in battle. To make it a trifecta, Philip's horses had also been victorious, winning at the Olympic Games. The queen decided that her son's birth, her husband's battle triumph, and Olympic laurels merited a personal response. So she gave herself a new name. Born Polyxena, she had named herself Myrtale when she joined a cult, but Alexander's mother is most commonly known as Olympias, the name taken in honor of the king's victory at the Olympic Games of 356 BCE.

All of which sounds worthy of celebration, but the truth is that Alexander's royal parents were a tempestuous pair. Had they lived in modern times, their marriage would have made the front pages of the tabloids. As it was, Philip's infidelities and Olympias' jealousy attracted sufficient notice to become notorious, creating reputations that have lasted for centuries.

Early Influences
As a royal prince, he was smart enough—the legendary philosopher Aristotle was his tutor from age 13 to 16 years—and privileged enough to have chosen an easier life had he wanted to do so. But nobility in those ancient times did not necessarily promise a life of ease. In order to maintain what he was destined to inherit, he would need to defend it. The tempo of the times also meant that a leader had to expect that his lands would be coveted by others; a nation which had a powerful military man on the throne seemed more likely to thrive.

Philip was a warrior, and he would expect his son to follow his lead. But Alexander's gifts were not merely military. From an early age Alexander became the stuff of legend, some coming from a time when it was easy to believe that a youth so gifted was surely the offspring of the gods, perhaps even Zeus himself (a tale that might have flattered Olympias, but not necessarily Philip), and others from the boy's own remarkable exploits.

Nearly as famous as Alexander is his horse. The story says that one day, a trader brought a horse to court to sell, but the horse refused to accept a rider. No one could mount him. Recognizing such a beast as useless for his purposes, King Philip lost interest. But ten-year old Alexander proved himself to be an observant boy; he had noticed that the horse was frightened of its own shadow. Through careful training, gaining the horse's trust, and patience unusual in a child of that age, Alexander was able to mount and ride him. This stamina and insight would serve him well as the horse Bucephalus bore his master into battle in lands far from Macedon.

At 16, Alexander's education ended. Aristotle had taught him, as well as the youths who would become his generals, well. Alexander himself was a voracious reader, but the Greek philosopher also taught his students lessons which reflected the broad and expansive regard for knowledge which was characteristic of the Athenians: they learned philosophy and logic, science, ethics, art, and medicine.

From the classroom, Alexander went to the battlefield, and when there was a revolt against the king, it was the king's son who put it down and named a city after himself, one of 70 that would bear his name. One of those cities would be Alexandria in Egypt, which would eventually be second in size only to Rome. Father and son went to war against their foes, defeating the Athenians and the Thebans and establishing an alliance with the intention of going to war against the mighty Persian Empire.

Father and son were brothers-in-arms, but as father and son, their relationship was often stormy. Alexander's position as heir depended upon his father's intention to keep him so, but also upon the absence of another claimant. Philip's marriage to a young woman of childbearing age brought those possibilities home when the bride's uncle, who also happened to be Philip's general, became drunk and, speaking unwisely, as wedding guests have done since time immemorial, voiced his hope that his niece would give birth to an heir. Not the kind of wedding toast that the current heir was likely to welcome. Alexander, along with his mother, Olympias, escaped from Macedon, but Alexander returned six months later when father and son had had time to calm down.

Alexander's Life Changes
Weddings were not lucky for Philip. As father of the bride, he was assassinated at his daughter's wedding by one of his bodyguards, leaving his son Alexander the undisputed heir at age 20. There is some belief that Alexander's mother was aware of the plot against her husband and was not opposed to becoming the widow of King Philip and the mother of King Alexander.

Claiming the throne was one thing; keeping it was another. First, Alexander had to clean house; that meant disposing of any potential rivals: family members, rival princes, and of course the rash general who had expressed his wish for a fertile marriage for the niece who had married Alexander's father.

That bloody duty accomplished, Alexander next turned his attentions to those conquered lands who thought that an untried youth would be easy to vanquish. The untried youth and his cavalry wasted no time in riding against the rebels. His shrewd strategy, remarkable in someone so young, brought the army to surrender. He defeated rebellious Thracians, Illyrians and Taulanti, then had to deal once again with Thebans and Athenians in revolt. Alexander had been injured during the siege of Pelium and the rumor of his death seemed credible enough, sufficiently credible to encourage Themes to revolt against their Macedonian overlords. Alexander had been relying on the presence of Macedonian troops to keep the Greeks in order, but he'd had to pull the troops when the Thracian and Illrian revolts erupted. But Alexander's military acumen was already showing its prowess as he travelled 300 miles within two weeks, miraculously bringing his army undetected to the site of the battle under the very noses of his Greek enemies.

Wary of the Macedonian's skills, Athens and Sparta decided to play a waiting game. Thebes voted for war. Alexander was prepared to be lenient; if Thebes turned over the two men who had incited the revolt, no one would be hurt. Thebes issued a counter offer which was refused. This time, Alexander taught Thebes a lesson that was not lost on the rest of Greece; he burned the city to the ground. Those Thebans who weren't killed in battle were sold as slaves.

Alexander might have had an elite education, but when it came to warfare, he was no schoolboy. The Macedonian was intent on conquest. Next stop: Persia.

King Darius III of Persia was ready for the battle, with an army of

149

perhaps as many as 200,000 soldiers to meet Alexander's 35,000 men (numbers are imprecise, but historians agree that Darius had a much larger force). With a tactical move that fooled the Persians into moving onto rocky terrain and away from the flat battlefield where they had the advantage, Alexander charged through the rear of the Persian army. Darius fled the battlefield. The conquest continued for several more years, but when Darius was killed in 330 BC, Alexander took his place as the Persian king. One more crown added to his collection.

He went on to conquer Egypt and Babylon. When his horse Bucephalus died in what today is Pakistan, Alexander named a city for him. Battle in India was to present a new threat in the form of war elephants. But once again, the Macedonians were triumphant. And weary.

At the Hyphasis River, the Macedonians told their ruler, their general, their companion, that they had had enough and would go no farther. Alexander was not pleased with their mutiny, and sulked in his quarters like Achilles. But they would not change their minds. When he agreed to turn back, the army broke out in cheers and shouts of joy.

The man who conquered the known world would not live long to enjoy his efforts. In June 323 BCE, he attended a banquet and along with the other guests, took part in the bouts of drinking that followed. Feeling unwell, he went to bed, his condition worsening. Realizing that he was mortally ill, his soldiers wanted to see him for one last time. Although he didn't speak, he nonetheless acknowledged with a nod or a glance the soldiers of his army as they came to him. Ten days later, with a fever sapping his strength, Alexander died at the age of 33. Given the sanitary conditions of the times, historians deduce that the cause of death might have been typhoid fever or malaria. Of course, given the political climate of the era, it might also have been poison.

Alexander had spent his adult life in conquest, acquiring lands so that he could rule them and consolidate individual nations into one empire. But his death brought an end to the dreams of lasting empire. He had married three times; his child by Roxana of Bactria, Alexander IV of Macedon, was born six months after Alexander's death. Roxana, ambitious to secure her unborn child's position as heir, had her rival wives murdered. Her efforts were futile, as Alexander IV was murdered within a few years, and the empire divided up among Alexander the Great's generals.

Why Alexander Matters

Ptolemy, one of those generals, brought Alexander's body to Alexandria, where his tomb became a favorite destination for travelers of the ancient world, including Julius Caesar. The library at Alexandria was a great center of learning that celebrated the achievements of the Greeks and was a prized asset of the intellectual community until it was burned, centuries after Alexander's death.

Although the Greeks were conquered by the Macedonian father and son, Greek culture triumphed, and Alexander made no attempt to subdue it; he had a great regard for the sophisticated accomplishments of the Greeks. He brought his armies to the lands he conquered, but the spread of Greek culture would prove to be more enduring than his rule. Hellenistic ideals, philosophy, and learning, consolidated by the wandering conqueror, spread far across the subjugated lands. Western thought would be heavily influenced by the intellectual legacy of the Greeks. The

151

three thousand miles of land that he claimed would become an ancient global community where trade and learning flourished.

[Excerpt from the first 2 Chapters]

77120108R00086

Made in the USA
Middletown, DE
17 June 2018